Walking the Edo Sanpu

Also by William de Lange

A Fool's Journey
A Fool's Return
Samurai Battles
Samurai Sieges
Samurai Dishes
Miyamoto Musashi
Musashi: Fact & Fiction
The Real Musashi, I, II, III
Famous Samurai, I, II, III
The Remarkable History of the Yagyū Clan
An Encyclopedia of Japanese Castles
The Namamugi Incident
A History of Japanese Journalism
A Dictionary of Japanese Onomatopoeia
A Dictionary of Japanese Proverbs
A Dictionary of Japanese Idioms
Japan Then & Now
Japanese Scrolls
Pars Japonica
Iaido

WALKING THE EDO SANPU

Nagasaki to Tokyo in Dutch Footsteps

William de Lange

For Yoko Odaka & Kees van der Meer

For more on books by William de Lange visit:
www.williamdelange.com

First edition, 2024

Published by TOYO PRess
Visit us at: **www.toyopress.com**

Copyright © 2024 by William de Lange

ISBN: 978-94-92722-45-4

Table of Content

Yo no naka wa
munashiki mono to
shiru toki shi
yoyo masumasu
kanashikarikeri

When I realize
just how fragile
this world truly is,
Then all the more
am I struck with sadnesss.

— Ōtomo no Tabito (665–731)

Introduction

The Liefde

When, in 1636, *Shōgun* Tokugawa Iemitsu (1604–51) banned all Portuguese and Spaniards from entering Japan on the punishment of death, the only foreigners left to trade with Japan except the Chinese were the Dutch. For the next two-and-a-half centuries, the Dutch trading post on the fan-shaped island of Dejima in the Bay of Nagasaki would be Japan's sole window on the West.

The Dutch first arrived in Japan in 1600 when, on 20 April, the Dutch merchantman *Liefde* (*Love*) cast its anchor near the small island of Kuroshima on the north side of Usuki Bay on the northeast coast of Japan's southern island of Kyushu. It was a miracle her crew had the power to even drop the anchor—what was left of them, that is. Of the one hundred and ten able hands who had boarded her at the mouth of the Maas near Rotterdam on June 27 two years earlier, only twenty-four were still alive when the badly mauled vessel limped into Usuki Bay. Six more would die before the month was out. By that time, the *Liefde* had been towed into the nearby port of Usuki by its lord, *Daimyō* Ōta Shigemasa (d. 1617), who confiscated her cargo and incarcerated her crew.

The *Liefde* had never intended to sail for Japan. She had been part of an expedition of five ships that sailed for the East Indies in the hope of copying the example of Cornelis de Houtman, who had returned from the Spice Islands three years earlier with the coveted commodities of pepper and nutmeg. In the end, only one of the five ships would ever reach its destination. The chief reason for the disaster had been their decision to do so by passing through the treacherous Strait of Magellan. Adverse winds had forced them to overwinter within the strait, causing more than a hundred of their crews to perish from cold and starvation. One ship, the *Gheloove* (*Faith*) returned home, her crew cut down to a third. Another, the

The five Dutch ships, ready to set sail from Rotterdam

Blijde Bootschap (*Gospel*) was captured by the Spanish off Valparaiso. Even the *Trouwe* (*Fidelity*), the one vessel that did reach the spice islands of Ternate and Tidore, met with disaster when her crew was invited ashore by the Portuguese and slaughtered, almost to a man. Just six of them survived, only three of whom made it back home.

The *Liefde*, so one of its survivors told Lord Shigemasa, had eventually ended up following a more northerly course across the

Pacific. Having lost sight of the rest of the fleet after they had exited the Strait of Magellan and dispersed in a violent storm, she and one other ship, the *Hoope* (*Hope*), had initially set sail for Santa Maria, the point of rendezvous in the event of a calamity. But when, after two months of waiting, the others failed to arrive, the ship's council decided to sail on without them. And thus, on 27 November 1599, they had 'stood away directly for Japan.' The first part of the Pacific crossing had been favorable and they had 'passed the equinoctial line with a fair wind.' By late January 1600, they had called at the Mariana Islands, where eight of their remaining sixty men fled ashore in a stolen pinnacle. They pursued their crossing without them, until, on 23 February, they ran into 'a wondrous storm of wind' in which they 'lost our consort, whereof we were very sorry.'

Shigemasa's interlocutor was not a Dutchman. Like most of the rest of the *Liefde*'s crew, the ship's captain, Jacob Quackernaeck, was on the brink of death. One of the few men still able to go about was an Englishman, a man by the name of William Adams, the *Liefde*'s pilot. He also had a reasonable command of Portuguese and was thus able to answer the questions put to him through Padre João Rodríguez, who ran a Jesuit Mission in nearby Funai and happened to be visiting Usuki at the time of the *Liefde*'s arrival. It was Adams' relative good health, his ability to communicate with the Japanese, and his position as the *Liefde*'s second in command, that made the governor of Nagasaki, Terazawa Hirotaka (1563–1633), the highest authority on the island, decide to single the Englishman out to represent the Dutch case to the highest authority in the realm: Tokugawa Ieyasu, then still the head of the *Gotairō*, the Council of five Elders that had been called into life by Toyotomi Hideyoshi to ensure the succession of his infant son Hideyori.

And so it was that, on 12 May 1600, Adams was brought to the northern wing of Osaka Castle for an audience with Ieyasu. He was met by two officials, who led the pilot into a large matted room, where all three of them sat down cross-legged. At length, upon some signal, the two men rose and led Adams to another room. In it, seated on a slight elevation, sat Tokugawa Ieyasu, resting one arm leisurely on a lacquered armrest and raising the other, beckoning the pilot to

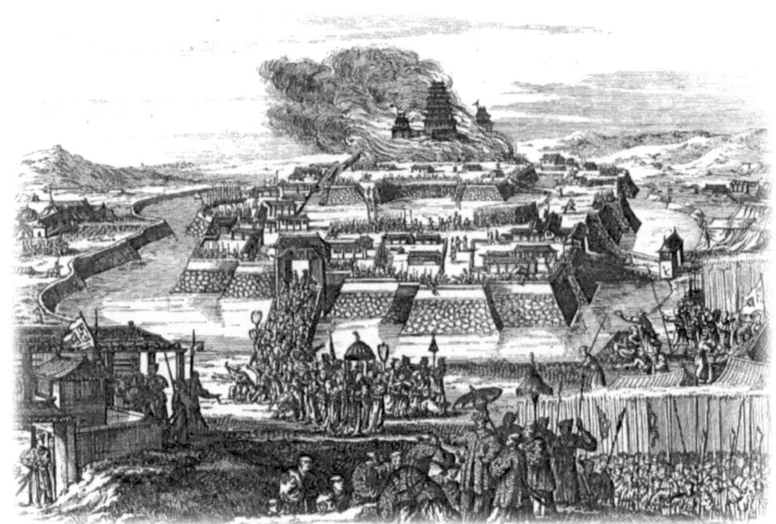

Osaka Castle during the siege in 1615

come closer. The ruler omitted all forms of ceremony and immediately began to question Adams by means of signs, some of which the pilot understood and some he did not. Yet despite the limitations of their exchange, and to Adams' considerable relief, he 'viewed me well, and seemed to be wonderfull favorable.' It had clearly been with a view to form such an impression independently, without the aid of any foreign interpreter, that Ieyasu had chosen to subject Adams to this mode of questioning; for presently the two men were joined by a Portuguese interpreter through which the regent asked Adams 'of what land I was, and what moved us to come to his land, being so far off.' Having brought with him some of the sea charts on board the *Liefde*, Adams 'showed unto him the name of our country,' and explained 'that our land had long sought out the East Indies, and desired friendship with all Kings and potentates in way of merchandise, having in our land diverse commodities, which these lands had not: and also to buy such merchandise in this land, which our country had not.' Ieyasu did not pursue the matter any further but now wanted to know 'whether our country had warres.' Adams acknowledged that the Netherlands was indeed at war with Spain and Portugal, but stressed that it was 'in peace with all other nations.' Asked in what did he believe, he replied 'in God, that made heaven and earth.'

The rest of the day was spent in much the same fashion; whilst Adams marveled at the opulence of his new surroundings, a 'wonderful costly house gilded with gold in abundance,' the ruler bombarded the pilot with questions:

> He asked me diverse other questions of things of religion, and many other things: As what way we came to the country. Hauing a chart of the whole world, I shewed him, through the Straight of Magellan. At which he wondred, and thought me to lie. Thus from one thing to another, I abode with him till mid-night. And hauing asked mee, what merchandize we had in our shippe, I shewed him all. In the end, he being ready to depart, I desired that we might haue trade of merchandize, as the Portugals and Spanyards had.

Ieyasu can't have been too convinced by Adams' claim the Dutch had come to trade. Their vessel, so he had been informed by the governor of Nagasaki, 'did not carry goods in such quality or of the same quality as brought by the other vessels that came to Japan.' Nor had her crew 'come well dressed, splendid with the pomp of servants and attendants as the other merchants were accustomed to come, but rather as soldiers and sailors, and besides with much ordinance and arms.' But Ieyasu wasn't very interested in the Dutch merchandise; his interest lay with their ordinance and arms. And going by the governor's inventory of the ship's cargo, the latter two commodities were present in substantial quantities. Besides some chests of coral, amber, glass beads, and woolen cloth, he had found 'nineteen large bronze pieces of ordnance and other small ones, five hundred muskets, and five thousand balls of cast iron.

To Ieyasu, the arrival of the Dutch could not have come at a better time, for Japan was not a country at peace. For more than a century she had been torn by internal strife. More recently, large parts of the country had been pacified: first under Oda Nobunaga, who had brought central Japan under his control; then by Toyotomi Hideyoshi, who had subdued the north and west of Honshu, as well as Shikoku and Kyushu. Ieyasu had forged a pact with both men at different junctures, helping them to achieve their aim of uniting the country. Now Hideyoshi was dead, and, being the head of the *Gotairō*, he was determined to complete their mission. But a large number of chieftains, mainly in Japan's western provinces, opposed his ascendancy. They had coalesced around Ishida Mitsunari, one of the *Gobugyō*, the Five Commissioners, another organ meant to ensure Hideyori's succession. From the moment Hideyoshi passed away, Ieyasu and Mitsunari had been engaged in a struggle for power. The standoff had come to a head two months earlier, when Mitsunari resigned from the Go*bugyō* in a fit of anger and returned to his headquarters of Wakayama Castle on the southeast shore of Lake Biwa. From there, so Ieyasu's spies told him, he was orchestrating a growing coalition against Ieyasu's authority, casting aspersions on his loyalty to the house of Toyotomi. The Dutch ordinance and arms, then, Ieyasu was sure, would stand him in good stead in the inevitable

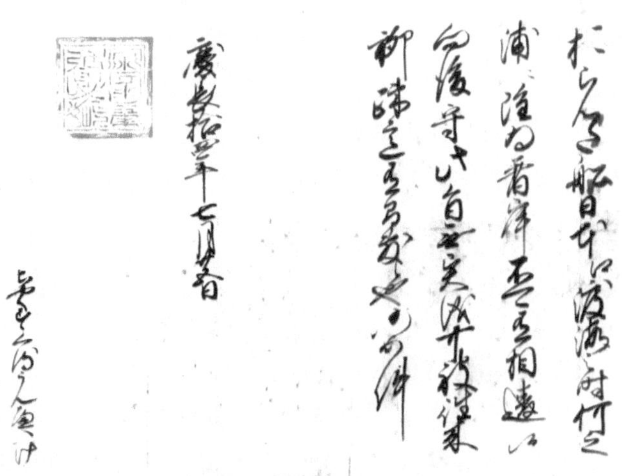

Iewyasu's red-seal passport for the Dutch

showdown between his eastern forces and the western chieftains.

And so, the Dutch were allowed to stay. Nine years later, on 14 August 1609, the Dutch ambassadors Jacob van den Broeck (?–?), Nicolaes Puyck (?–?), and Melchior van Santvoort (1570–1641) crossed the East Gate of Sunpu Castle in Fuchū (Shizuoka City) for an audience with Tokugawa Ieyasu. The sixty-six-year-old man showed himself 'very pleased' with the gifts of raw silk. Even the bars of lead were accepted with good grace. Particularly gratifying to the Japanese ruler seemed a letter from Prince Maurits van Oranje (1567–1625). It was not without effect. Ten days later, the ambassadors were again called to Sunpu Castle, where the potentate presented them with a beautifully ornamented Japanese sword, a written reply to the prince, and a red-seal passport stating that 'Whenever Dutch ships come to Japan, they shall be refused by no one, at whatever port they may arrive. So in future, shall this commandment be observed, and they shall be able to come and go as they please, without any hindrance whatsoever.'

Dejima

Up to this day, Ieyasu's red-seal passport has in effect remained in place, the one exception being the war years. The document's sell-by date proved less effective when it came to the ports at which the Dutch were allowed to call. Already in 1616, the year of Ieyasu's death, the Dutch (and for a short while the` English) were forced to limit their trade to the port of Hirado, just off Kyushu's west coast.

For the next two decades, the Dutch conducted their trade from Hirado's roadstead. It was a profitable trade. By 1639, eleven Dutch merchantmen entered Hirado Bay, carrying a total cargo valued at close to four million guilders ($53 million in today's money). The next year, the annual number of ships had risen to thirteen while the total value of imports rose to six million guilders. That same year, the Dutch celebrated the completion of a new, expanded Dutch factory with an inscription on one of the building's crossbeams. The text seemed innocent enough: 'AD 1640' it read. Not to the Japanese authorities, who took offense at the Dutch counting their years according to the Christian Era. They had just crushed a Christian rebellion on the nearby Shimabara Peninsula, where some twenty thousand believers had ensconced themselves in an abandoned stronghold called Hara Castle. It had taken more than a hundred thousand troops and four months of fighting to reduce the stronghold. Indeed, even the Dutch had been called upon the

The Dutch factory in Hirado

bombard the rebels, which they duly did, lobbing close to four hundred shells into the fortress from one of their ships and a hastily improvised shore battery. Their rendered services did not make up for the offending crossbeam. François Caron, the then factor was instructed to again tear down his factory, brick by brick, beam by beam, in the exact same order in which they had been laid.

In truth, what would now be called 'Crossbeam–Gate' was just a pretext. The *bakufu* wanted the Dutch out, not out of Japan but out of Hirado. They had a far better alternative: Dejima, an artificial island in the Bay of Nagasaki. It had been built to house the Portuguese. That setup had fallen through when, on 5 July 1639, Portuguese ships were banned from entering Japanese ports. The *bakufu* elders had had enough of their missionaries, who in their mind were the cause of the rebellion. Now the island lay vacant. And what

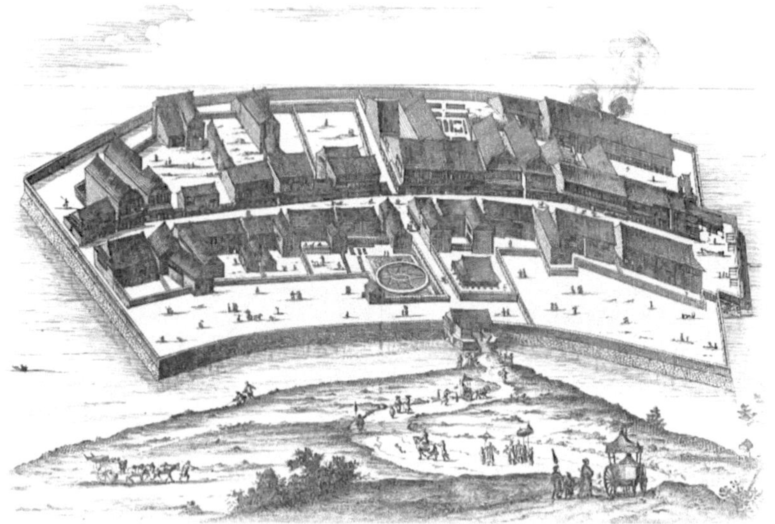

Dejima Island and the new Dutch factory

better way to put the island to good use than to house the Dutch there? In that way, they would have a safe port of call in the well-protected and spacious Bay of Nagasaki, immediately in front of the large port of Nagasaki, which sat at the terminus of the Nagasaki Kaidō, Kyushu's main high road. For the *bakufu*, it was safer, too, though for different reasons. They now had the Dutch nicely assembled within a small and confined space where the governor of

Nagasaki could keep a close eye on them. It was a no-brainer, a win-win situation.

No buildings to house the Dutch had yet been erected, so the Japanese architects approached the Dutch to teach them their building methods. This they did. They suggested using bricks and mortar for the warehouses, which would make them more resistant to fire than the plaster and wood of Japanese buildings. The Japanese architects agreed, but when they applied for permission from the *bakufu* the request was turned down. Bricks, the *bakufu* argued, might be fire-proof, but they weren't earthquake-proof.

Dejima's construction was a costly affair; it set the builders back by some four thousand *ryō* (roughly $2.7 million in today's money). On top of that came another two thousand *ryō* for the wood-and-plaster buildings. The largest chunk of the financial burden was borne by the *bakufu*; they financed the island, its stone walls, the bridge to the mainland, and the gate at its end. The cost for the buildings and the rest was borne by a consortium of twenty-five Nagasaki bigwigs, who recouped their investment in the form of an annual rent to the tune of sixteen hundred *ryō*. Initially, the rent was levied on the Portuguese. After the Dutch moved in, in 1641, the then-factor Maximiliaan le Maire (1606–54) managed to whittle it down to eleven hundred.

Sankin Kōtai

The Dutch referred to their factor as *opperhoofd*, or 'chief;' the Japanese considered him a *'capitan.'* And since the Dutch *opperhoofd* ruled over his own little kingdom of Dejima Island, the *bakufu* decided to give him some of the same prerogatives and duties reserved for *daimyō*, the feudal lords in charge of Japan's two hundred and fifty-odd domains. Those prerogatives and duties came together in a ritual known as the Edo Sanpu, or 'visiting the metropole of Edo.' It was the annual duty of going up to Edo to have an audience with the *shōgun* and show one's loyalty. It wasn't a new thing. Ever since the Kamakura period (1185–1333), local chieftains had been expected to

*Daimyō mansions (*yashiki*) in Edo*

show their allegiance to the *bakufu*. It was only after 1635 that, on Tokugawa Iemitsu's orders, it became a biannual duty for all of Japan's *daimyō*. Known as the *sankin kōtai*, or the system of 'alternate attendance,' a *daimyō* was obliged to maintain a large mansion in the shadow of Edo Castle. There he had to spend one year with his womenfolk and offspring, taking on various duties (such as guarding the castle and running Edo's fire brigade) and having his audience with the *shōgun*. When the year was up, he could return to his domain and ensure his elders weren't neglecting their duties. There was just one proviso: he had to leave his spouse and heir behind. It was a brilliant system, really. The huge costs of maintaining his luxurious mansion in Daimyōkoji—something like today's Bell Air or Palm Island—helped to ensure he would have a hard time raising troops in revolt; the virtual hostage-taking of his wife and son meant he would think twice before he would even consider such a move.

Dutch *opperhoofd*s had already been doing the Edo Sanpu well before Tokugawa Iemitsu made it a fixed ritual. From the moment the Dutch set up shop in Hirado they undertook what they referred to as the *hofreis*, or the 'court journey,' though not every year. The route the early Missions took was different, too. The first leg of the journey, from Nagasaki to the port of Shimonoseki at the western tip of the main island of Honshu, was made over sea. There they would board a vessel with a crew that knew how to navigate Japan's Inland Sea and arrive at the metropole of Osaka. After that, they continued their journey over land via Kyoto to Edo along the old Tōkaidō high road. Yet the dangerous trip around Kyushu's jagged and exposed west coast proved too much of a hindrance and, from 1659 onward, the first leg of the journey was made overland along the Nagasaki Kaidō. Part of it was still done over water, across the wide Bay of Ōmura, which shortened the distance by several dozen miles, but only if the weather allowed. The overland route had its own hurdles, the main one being the Hiyamizu Pass, just east of present-day Fukuoka City. From there, it was downhill to the port of Kokura on Kyushu's north coast, from where they would cross the Strait of Shimonoseki to board the vessel that, as before, would carry the Mission across the Inland Sea.

The early Missions departed from Nagasaki in the fall to arrive in Edo around the New Year. But from 1661 onwards, Missions tended to depart from Nagasaki around New Year's Day to arrive in Edo before March—according to Japan's lunisolar calendar, that is. Thus the Mission in which the German physician Engelbert Kaempfer traveled departed from Nagasaki on 14 February 1691 according to the Western, Gregorian calendar, but on the 17th of the 1st month of the 4th year of the Genroku era (1688–1704) according to the Japanese, lunisolar calendar; it arrived in Edo on Tuesday 13 March according to the Western calendar, but on the 24th day of the 2nd month according to the Japanese, well in time for the beginning of March.

There was a reason why the Dutch mission had to be in Edo around the New Year and, from the middle of the 17th century onward, before the beginning of March. New Year's Day was one of the designated days on which those *daimyō* whose turn it was to have an audience with the *shōgun* had to go up to Edo Castle. The 3rd day of March, too, was such a day. It was the second of the so-called *Gosekku*, the 'five seasonal festivals': 7 January, Mankind's Day or the Feast of the Seven Herbs (*Jinjitsu*); 3 March, Girl's Day or Doll Festival (*Jōshi*); 5 May, Boy's Day (*Tango*); 7 July, Seventh Night or Star Festival (*Shichiseki*); 9 September, Chrysanthemum Festival (*Chōyō*). The same was true of the 1st and the 15th day of the month. On all of these days, the grounds of Edo Castle would be swarming with the large processions of *daimyō* waiting their turn to enter the castle's inner citadel and have their audience with the *shōgun* and celebrate the day's festivities. Thus, on 3 March (according to the lunisolar calendar), it being Doll Festival, the interiors of the *Shōgun*'s huge residence within Edo Castle's inner citadel were festooned with *hinaningyō*, small dolls that are even today used to celebrate Girl's

Day. As can be imagined, with dozens and dozens of *daimyō* waiting their turn to enter the castle's inner citadel to visit the *shōgun*, to have the Dutch mingle with them was not desirable. But the *shōgun* and his court did want to meet the Dutch *opperhoofd* when the inner court of Edo Castle was set up for such a reception, so that they had to arrive in Edo around these dates.

On their one-thousand-mile journey to Edo, the Mission would spend the night at one of the post towns along the major traffic routes. All of Japan's high roads had such post towns. The origins of the Japanese post town system went all the way back to the Nara period (710–794), when in the image of mainland China, the Japanese imperial court established the first high road system with government-run post stations. Covering much of inhabited Japan, it stretched for a total of more than five thousand miles and had some four hundred post stations (*eki*) at ten-mile intervals. Though the system fell into disrepair during Japan's long period of civil strife, it was revamped during the peaceful Edo period (1603–1868), when the Tokugawa *bakufu* established the so-called *go-kaidō*, or the 'five high roads.' These five high roads—the Tōkaidō, the Nikkō Kaidō, the Okushū Kaidō, the Kōshū Kaidō, and the Nakasendō—connected the corners of the realm to the de-facto capital of Edo, where they converged at the node of the Nihonbashi Bridge, just east of Edo Castle. Like under the old high road system, the Edo-period high roads had post stations at regular intervals, with post-horses, personnel, and inns for dignitaries and commoners alike.

Just like the rest of Japan's feudal society, there was a strict hierarchy in the type of inns that could be found at a high road's post towns, especially the larger ones. At the top of the scale sat the *honjin*, the official accommodations for *daimyō* and other dignitaries like imperial and shogunal messengers. These establishments were well-equipped with special guest rooms where dignitaries could receive guests during their stay. The senior retainers who accompanied them were usually put up at the *waki-honjin* or 'side-*honjin*,' which usually adjoined the main accommodation but were less luxurious and able to put up more guests. All other travelers had to make do with *hatago*, the regular inns that put you up for the night and served evening meals and breakfasts. Given that, at any time, dozens of *daimyō* were underway to or from Edo, along with merchants, pilgrims, and even tourists, the demand for accommodations at these post towns was high. Thus the post town of Odawara alone had close to a hundred inns.

Since the *opperhoofd* had effectively the same status as a *daimyō*, he and his entourage generally stayed at *honjin*. Four inns along the way to Edo were invariably frequented by the Dutch and therefore also known among local Japanese as Oranda-*juku*: the Ōsaka-*ya* in Kokura, the Nagasaki-*ya* in Osaka, the Ebi-*ya* in Kyoto, and the Nagasaki-*ya* in Edo. A particularly special treatment was provided by the *toshiyori*, or 'town elders.' of the port of Shimonoseki. Two families, the Sakō and the Itō, took hereditary turns in filling the post of mare of this important port and logistical hub, and it seems that both families were passionate Holandophiles, who put the members of the Mission up in their own residences.

Missions

Going just by their Dutch participants, the Missions that embarked on the Edo Sanpu were a modest affair, just the *opperhoofd*s, accompanied by a scribe and a physician. It was, after all, not necessarily a diplomatic mission (as Melchior van Santvoort's to Ieyasu at Sunpu Castle had been) but rather an embassy of obeisance, an annual display of loyalty that ensured the Dutch retained their position of most favored (trading) nation. Of course, Dejima's *opperhoofd* did not really represent the Dutch nation as such but rather the Dutch East India Company, the world's first joint-stock company. In many ways there was little difference between the two: the VOC had powers many a modern-day multinational would drool over: its Lord Seventeen could imprison and execute convicts, negotiate treaties with other nations, establish colonies, and even wage wars to acquire them. As their representative, the *opperhoofd* would have been a pretty powerful chap elsewhere. Not in Japan. There, the only power he swayed was over his small staff of merchants, scribes, and domestics who kept the trading post going.

Yet since the Japanese treated the *opperhoofd* as a *daimyō* of sorts, the escort he received on his way to Edo was still impressive. It included an inspector and assistant inspector from Nagasaki's governor's office, a small army of senior, junior, and apprentice interpreters, several clerks, physicians, cooks, guards, treasurers, various runners and assistants, and a small army of porters. In all, a train of some sixty men accompanied the three foreigners on their trip, ensuring their safety and seeing to their daily needs and wishes. It might seem much, but it paled into insignificance when compared to the escorts of proper *daimyō*, which could number anywhere between a few hundred to a few thousand men. Thus the escort that, in 1841, accompanied Maeda Nariyasu (1811–84), the lord of the Kaga domain in Japan's Hokuriku region, a domain that covered the better part of three provinces, counted 1639 samurai, 2337 porters, and 103 horses. The trains of such escorts could span several miles so that its head might have arrived at the next post town while its tail still lingered in the previous one.

In the course of their more than two centuries of confinement on Dejima, the Dutch embarked on a total of 167 Edo Sanpu. It would have been more had Dutch trade with Japan not dwindled toward the end of the 18th century, as a result of which (after 1790) the

18th-century Dutch engraving depicting the Edo Sanpu

opperhoofd only had to visit Edo every four years. The last *opperhoofd* to make the journey was Janus Henricus Donker Curtius (1813–79), who, in 1856, visited *Shōgun* Tokugawa Iesada (1824–58) to conclude the Dutch-Japanese Friendship Treaty, opening the port of Nagasaki up to free Dutch trade and making Dejima a thing of the past.

Only a small number of the men—sadly, women were not allowed— who participated in the Dutch missions to Edo took the trouble to

xxvi

record their experiences, often in the form of diaries. One such man was Dirk de Graeff van Polsbroek (1833–1916). Polsbroek was a man of considerable social standing back home. Born into a family of aristocratic descent, he began his diplomatic career as an assistant to the Dutch trading station in Batavia. There, he gradually climbed the ranks until, in 1857, he was sent to Japan to serve Donker Curtius as a scribe at the Dutch factory on Dejima. It was in the same capacity

Van Polsbroek (right) and a colleague with Japanese guards in Edo

that he accompanied Donker Curtius on his second Mission to Edo a year later to renegotiate the Dutch-Japanese Friendship Treaty when (as a result of Commodore Matthew Calbraith Perry's gunboat diplomacy) the Americans obtained far more favorable conditions with their Treaty of Amity and Commerce.

Van Polsbroek wasn't a keen traveler, at least not where it concerned Japan. A walk through Shimonoseki 'yielded nothing,'

Kyoto was left behind 'without any regret,' and Edo turned out to be 'a disappointment.' But then again, he hadn't been keen on leaving Dejima in the first place, as he 'had so much hoped to finally get some rest, but there you go!'

Not all was doom and gloom with Van Polsbroek; he did at times manage to muster some enthusiasm. At Hyōgo, for instance, where both he and Donker Curtius were 'delighted with this large and prosperous city and its handsome anchorage, and we spoke as with one voice when we said that the city should be opened for European trade.' Or at Hara, where the factor and scribe were invited to visit the (still extant) Taishō-*en*, a botanical garden visited by the members of almost all Missions during the first half of the 19th century. It was founded by Kaihō Seiryō (1755–1817), a Confucianist scholar who had eloped from his native domain of Miyazu north of Kyoto to travel the length and breadth of the country to promote his Confucian-inspired policy on how to reinvigorate the economies of Japan's failing domains. Not that Van Polsbroek was aware of all this; he believed Seiryō to be a 'wealthy merchant.' But he was quite enamored when, having visited the gardens, he and the factor

> were invited to the man's house and received by his wife, his twenty-three-year-old son and his wife, and their fifteen-year-old daughter, who were as thoroughly decent, friendly, and civil as one could wish for. Both of us were enchanted by this loving ensemble and took our leave amid expressions of heartfelt gratitude.

Van Polsbroek's rapturous mood hadn't yet worn off when, the next day, he traversed the Hakone Pass:

Beautiful, vast, and truly impressive were the views. The populated hills and valleys below, the green spruce trees high up in the mountains, and the shimmering white dome of Fuji-*yama* beyond—in a word, produced such a delightful and wonderful scenery that we were left utterly speechless.

He wasn't a bigot either. Far from it. His view of Japan under *bakufu* rule and its future were both pertinent and prescient:

If the laws of Japan were less harsh and allowed its people to manufacture what they wanted, then the Japanese, equipped with the right examples, would assuredly be able to compete with Western industry. Currently, however, their industry is too much curtailed; the Japanese are not allowed to use the things they can do without [in the eyes of the authorities]. The policy of the Japanese government is to keep the populace under its thumb, and its civil servants and officers are subject to harsh discipline. By following this policy, Japan has known peace and quiet for more than 250 years. And now, we Europeans, hand in velvet glove, are to sign with them treaties of trade and amity. Our civilization, our religion, is to be imposed on this peaceable people, a people that, to my mind, is more civilized than any one of Europe's peoples. It hurts me to think of the consequences our intrusion will have for this country and its people. *Qui vivra, verra.*

Time has told indeed.

Another scribe to keep a journal of his journey to Edo was Johannes Gerhard Frederik van Overmeer Fischer (1800–48). The son of the mare of Harderwijk, similarly embarked for the Dutch East Indies to carve out a career for himself, doing so at the young age of seventeen after both his parents passed away. Appointed as a junior clerk in Batavia, he also gradually worked himself up until, around the age of twenty, he was sent on to Japan. There, he attained the position of 1st clerk, in which capacity he accompanied the Dutch factor to Edo in 1822. Compared to his aristocratic colleague's diary, Fischer's diary stands out for its author's curiosity: about the local trade, about the local history, about the local customs, superstitions, and traditions, about the local people—even a nonagenarian they happen to encounter during a stroll outside the village of Sonogi is of interest to Fischer. And he is pleasantly surprised to find that his curiosity is reciprocated:

> Of particular interest is the sheer number of scholars that can be found in the capital [sic.] of Edo, who understand the Dutch language and who, in their studies, resort to Dutch works. Among others, medicine, chemistry, astronomy, and physics are some of the most cherished disciplines, evidence of which is provided by the fact that the Japanese have translated into their language wholly or in part the medical works of Boerhaave, Van Gesscher, and Plenck, the *Batavian Apothecary*, Chomel's *Family Dictionary*, and the *Textbook on Physics* by Mr. J. Buis.

Fischer's ambition to broaden his understanding of Japan and its people and to share his insights with the people back home is borne out by the kind of book into which he cast his diary upon his return to The Netherlands in 1830. Published three years later by

Amsterdam's Muller & Company under the title *Bijdrage tot de Kennis van het Japansche Rijk* (*Contribution to the Knowledge of the Japanese Empire*), the 320-page work covers a lot more ground than just his journey to Edo. Japan's geography, its history, its sciences, its rarities, its art, its religion, its martial traditions, its flora and fauna—all, and much more besides, is covered in his ambitious work.

Fischer was also an avid collector. Penning the foreword to his book in Amsterdam in 1833, he explains how:

> My journey to the imperial capital [sic.] in the year 1822, and the friendly relationships I have been able to forge with sympathetic and capable Japanese, have enabled me to bring together a treasure trove of objects, which can open up a wide field of discovery and exploration for the diligent enthusiast of ethnology and other sciences.

Fischer's view was shared by the Dutch state, which purchased his collection lock stock and barrel and put it on display at The Hague's Mauritshuis.

Fischer was not the only one to keep a diary during his journey. It so happened that the Mission's head, *Opperhoofd* Jan Cock Blomhoff (1779–1853), also recorded his experiences in Japan, though not on the journey with Fisher in 1822 but during his previous Mission in 1818. Blomhoff started his career as a soldier. In 1794, at the age of fifteen, he took part as a cadet in Stadtholder Willem V's campaign to try and halt the French at Maastricht. When that campaign failed and the stadtholder went into exile in England, Blomhoff and his parents fled to Germany. There he joined a regiment of hunters in Osnabrück. It was with them that he later moved to England, only to eventually end up again in Bremen to try his luck as a trader. Meanwhile, the Netherlands lost its independence but regained peace; the Dutch Republic made place for the Batavian Republic ruled by Napoleon's younger brother Louis Napoléon Bonaparte. It did not keep Blomhoff from returning home in 1804, when he again entered the military, this time as lieutenant-adjutant under Herman Willem Daendels (1762–1818), the governor-general of the Dutch East

Blomhof and family with wetnurse (standing)

Indies, who shortly after sent the merchant-warrior onward to Japan to serve as warehouse keeper on Dejima under *Opperhoofd* Hendrik Doeff (1777–1835). Blomhoff left just in time to miss the capture of Batavia by the British. Being a French vassal state, the Dutch Republic was (like France) at war with Britain, which was making great inroads into the Dutch possessions in the Far East. Much of it was done under the direction of their colonial officer Sir Thomas

Stamford Binley Raffles (1781–1826). Having seized Java, he was now bent on also capturing the Dutch trading post on Dejima and, in 1813, dispatched two ships of war toward Japan. Daendels realized he needed to act and, aware of Blomhoff's martial and commercial acumen, ordered him back to Batavia to negotiate with the Brits. It was a bit of a disaster. Blomhoff was summarily taken prisoner and sent to Britain. Luckily for Blomhoff, by the time he arrived, the Brits and the Dutch had negotiated a treaty (the Anglo-Dutch Treaty of 1814). Released from captivity, he returned to the newly established Kingdom of the Netherlands, where King Willem I promptly knighted him Ridder in de Orde van de Nederlandse Leeuw for his 'steadfast refusal to surrender the Dutch factory on Dejima.' To ensure its future security and prosperity, he was sent to Japan to succeed Hendrik Doeff (1764–1837) as the new factor of Dejima. It was in that capacity that, in a concerted effort to tempt providence, Blomhoff and his then scribe, Hendrik Gerard Engelen, departed for their *hofreis* on Friday the 13th.

If Blomhoff's writing style is anything to go by, the man was a bit of a pompous git, invariably referring to himself in the 3rd person as 'Blomhoff,' or '*Opperhoofd*,' and even as 'the Hon'ble.' Not surprisingly, the Dutch knight in shining armor took considerable pride in noting how, on his way to what he (along with most other foreigners at the time) referred to as Japan's emperor, he—sorry, the Hon'ble—received the same treatment as the powerful *daimyō*:

All tokens of respect that are owed to the Japanese greats on their journey to the Emperor are also shown to the *Opperhoofd*. For this reason, several town servants, dressed and armed according to tradition, are sent ahead to summon the crowds along the road and to order them to prostrate themselves while the procession passes.

Otherwise, Blomhoff's record is bland, superficial, and chiefly concerned with the practical and logistical matters of the Mission: the number of porters, the availability and quality of the cooks, the (bad) weather, the (long) distances, the (poor) accommodations along the way, the (unpassable) rivers, and the long waits as a result of these impediments. As such, it gives a good impression of the conditions under which he managed to reach his destination, but it provides little insight into the country through which he passed, let alone the people he encountered. Concerned only with the Mission, his journal is also exceedingly short; a journey of a thousand miles that took him and his scribe more than four months to complete manages to fill only fifty-one pages.

Perhaps Blomhoff's best contribution (apart from keeping the increasingly unprofitable Dutch trade from collapsing altogether) was his collection of Japanese artifacts: coins, masks and whigs, costumes, luxury utensils, musical instruments, weapons, tools, woodwork and carvings, leatherwork, porcelain, lacquerware, paintings, writings—little escaped the factor's greedy little hands (see painting). Known today as the Blomhoff Collection, it was added to the Fischer Collection to form the core of the Japan collection of the National Museum of Ethnology in Leiden.

Remarkably, only few factors troubled themselves with chronicling their unique experiences. Or perhaps it wasn't that remarkable; the VOC was in Japan to make a profit, not to record or, heaven forbid, learn from its experiences in this remote neck of the woods, an attitude that Blomhoff's supercilious account exudes from all its pores.

What *is* remarkable is that it was some of the physicians who accompanied the *opperhoofd*s who were to leave the most fascinating and detailed accounts of the Dutch experience in Japan. Moreover, they weren't even Dutch but German. The earliest and most exhaustive account was penned down by the already mentioned German physician Engelbert Kaempfer (1651–1716). Kaempfer was an experienced traveler. In fact, his journey to Japan was the

Lemgo in Kaempfer's day

culmination of a decade-long journey that took him to Russia, Persia, India, Java, Siam, and finally to Japan.

Kaempfer was born in Lemgo, a small town in the Principality of Lippe, a small state in the Holy Roman Empire nestled between the Weser River and the Teutoburg Forest. His father was a pastor at the town's Church of S. Nicholas; his mother was the daughter of the Church's previous pastor. Despite this conservative background, the young Kaempfer enjoyed a liberal education, first at Hameln, then at Luneburg, then at Hamburg, then at Lubeck. It was a time in which he could let his precocious talents wander widely and freely into the fields of languages, history, geography, and even music. His constant moving around also betrayed a creative restlessness, a pattern that continued as he pursued his studies at Danzig, Thorn, Kraków, and finally at Königsberg in Prussia, where he buckled down and spent four years applying himself to the study of medicine and natural history. His first academic appointment came in 1861, when he became attached to the University of Uppsala in Sweden. Yet despite numerous offers to settle into a comfortable position he chose to satisfy his insatiable curiosity for things foreign: he wanted to travel.

It was while at the court of the Swedish king and patron of the sciences Karl XI, that Kaempfer met Samuel von Pufendorf, an early proponent of German Enlightenment, who helped him attain the position of secretary in the king's embassy to the court of Shah Suleiman I of Persia. Led by Ludvig Fabritius (1649–1729), a Dutchman with a colorful career in the Russian military, the embassy reached the Persian capital of Isfahan in 1684 by way of Moscow, Kazan, and Astrakhan. At Isfahan, Fabritius was offered a position in the Dutch East India Company but he turned it down to return to Sweden. Not so Kaempfer. Eager to see the Far East, he signed on with a Dutch fleet in the Persian Gulf as chief surgeon. Tracing the Arabian and Indian coasts, the fleet reached Batavia in 1689, and in the spring of the following year, Kaempfer embarked for Japan to become the chief physician at the Dutch trading post in Nagasaki.

Kaempfer spent just two years in Japan but they would be some of his most productive. Virtually no field of inquiry was left untouched in the explorer's quest to understand this fascinating country. One thing, however, the German was keen not to add:

> I inserted nothing created from my own fantasy, nothing that reeks of the writer's parlor, the study's lamp. I limited myself to only describing that which is either new or not thoroughly or fully handed down by others. As an explorer, I had no other aim than to gather observations of things that are not or not sufficiently known to us.

Presenting such a comprehensive view of such an incomprehensible country, Engelbert's work was destined to become a standard work, a touchstone for all who followed in his footsteps. And not only that. Ever since it first appeared in the early 18th century, it has inspired countless students of Japan and of the Far East in general. One of them was the author Jonathan Swift, who drew from Kaempfer's magical descriptions at the *shōgun*'s court to write his *Gulliver's Travels*. Kaempfer's manuscript, which was titled *Heutiges Japan*, is now available in English, Dutch, German, French, and Japanese, and has spawned a body of academic research on him and his writings that can fill a small library. Yet, incredibly enough, his groundbreaking work on Japan might never have been published had it not been for an enterprising Anglo-Irish physician. It was Hans Sloane—whose vast collection would form the foundation of the British Museum, the British Library, and London's Natural History Museum—who purchased Kaempfer's original manuscript along with the rest of his collection and writings.

Sloane instantly recognized the value of Kaempfer's work. He himself had published a similar work about the Caribbean in two volumes (*A Voyage to the Islands Madera, Barbados, Nieves, S. Christophers and Jamaica*), which he had written and published on his own strength following a voyage to the region on behalf of the Royal Society in 1687. Sloane was deeply impressed with the detail and scope of his German fellow-physician's work (which is now kept in the British Library). In the tradition of the time, that scope was reflected in the lengthy title under which, in 1727, Sloane (again on his own strength) had the work published in two folio volumes in London after it had been translated by the Swiss naturalist Johan Caspar Scheuchzer (1702–29). The full title ran: *The History of Japan, Giving an Account of the Ancient and Present State and Government of that Empire; Of Its Temples, Palaces, Castles, and other Buildings; Of Its Metals, Minerals, Trees, Plants, Animals, Birds and Fishes; Of The Chronology, and Succession of the Emperors, Ecclesiastical and Secular; Of The Original Descent, Religions, Customs, and Manufactures of the Natives; and of their Trade and Commerce with the Dutch and Chinese.* Sloane was thorough if nothing else; the work's subtitle read: *Together with a Description of the Kingdom of Siam, IV written in High-Dutch by Engelbertus Kaempfer, M.D., Physician to the Dutch Embassy to the Emperors Court; and translated from his Original Manuscript, never before printed, by J. G. Scheuckzer, F.R.S., and a Member of the College of Physicians, London. With the Life of the Author, and an Introduction. Illustrated with many Copper Plates.* Translating Kaempfer's tome probably killed the young Scheuchzer. Suffering from an already frail constitution, he died at the age of twenty-seven.

Sadly, Kaempfer never saw the work in print. He also did not live to see the first Dutch translation (from the English), which was published in Amsterdam in 1733 by Jan Roman de Jonge under the more modest title *De Beschrijving en geschiedenis van Japan* (*Description and History of Japan*). It would take until 1777 for the original German manuscript to be published in Lemgo by Christian Wilhelm von Dohm under the (reverse) title *Geschichte und Beschreibung von Japan*.

Having returned to Europe on the Dutch merchantman *Pampus* in 1693, Kaempfer initially traveled to Leiden, where he was awarded a doctorate in medicine at Leiden University. A year later, at the relatively young age of forty-three, he moved back to Germany, settling down at his father's Steinhof estate in his native town of Lemgo. In 1700, he married Maria Sophia Wilstach, the daughter of an eminent merchant from Stolzenau. It wasn't a happy marriage (he wrote her out of his will), nor was her dowry enough to support the family, which soon included a son and two daughters. To support his budding family, Kaempfer became the personal physician to Friedrich Adolf (1667–1718), the Count of Lippe-Detmold, a glut who spent most of his life building extravagant palaces and gardens, causing even the Russian Tsar Peter the Great to conclude his visit to Bad Pyrmont with the words: 'Your Highness is too big for his country.' It seems the earl relied heavily on Kaempfer's medical support, for he outlived his physician by little more than a year. It was a shame, really, that this man who had so much to offer the world would have to pour so much energy into a man who was more of a burden than a benefit to his people. Taxed by his duties to Count Adolf, tormented by the premature deaths of his three children, and afflicted by ill health, Kaempfer struggled on, using the little free time he had to organize and publish his extensive writings. When he finally passed away, on 12 November 1716, only one of his works, the *Amoenitates exoticae*, the chronicle of his Persian travels, had been published; the rest remained unorganized, much of it scattered among drawers and cabinets in his family estate. It was only through the effort of Johann

Georg Steigerthal (1666–1740), a member of the Royal Society who traveled down to Lippe and acquired Kaempfer's work on behalf of Hans Sloane (by now president of the Royal Society), that Kaempfer was saved from obscurity.

One of the men to carefully study Kaempfer's work was his fellow countryman Philipp Franz Balthasar von Siebold (1796–1866). Like Fischer, Siebold does not try to hide his sources. How could he? At every turn of the journey, Kaempfer's influence is felt in Siebold's work, if not in setting the scene, then in his choice of topic. Compare, for instance, the following two passages describing the castle town of Saga:

Kaempfer:

> This city is very large, but extends more in length than in breadth. It is exceedingly populous. Both going in and coming out, we found strong guards at the gates. It is enclosed with walls and gates, but more for state than defense. The streets are large, running straight east and south, with channels and rivers running through, which lose their waters into the Sea of Arima, as they call it, near a place of that name. The houses are but sorry and low, and, in the chief streets, fitted up for manufactures and shopkeepers.

Siebold:

> This large, populous city, which is perhaps the largest in Kyushu, measures 2 *ri* in length and 1 *ri* in width when one includes its outskirts. Its numerous streets cross each other at regular intervals according to the four wind directions. The

main street through which we passed, is broad and well kept, the houses, partly occupied by shopkeepers, partly by manufacturers, are low and sorry.

Of course, it is not fair to look at Siebold's work in this light. He openly acknowledges the towering example set by his predecessor, and far from wanting to copy him, he is keen to confirm, complement, or at most correct Kaempfer's observations. Besides, both men followed the almost same route, stopped at the same places, were made to visit the same sights, and were fed the same hackneyed stories by their native companions and hosts. It was inevitable that there should arise an overlap in their work.

In one respect, Siebold's work stands out from all others: its eye for Japan's flora and fauna. The reason for this is simple; Siebold was an avid botanist, even though, like Kaempfer, he was a trained physician. He was the son of Georg Christoph Siebold (1767–98), a medical professor at Würzburg's renowned Juliusspitals, and the grandson of Carl Caspar von Siebold (1736–1807), a towering intellect who not only founded the hospital but is also—at least in Germany— considered to be the founder of modern surgery.

Much more than Kaempfer, then, Siebold was destined to become a physician. And this he did, reading medicine at Würzburg's Julian Maximilian University, though he also acquired a *gründliches wissen*, a 'thorough knowledge' of botany, natural science, geography, and ethnology. Following a short stint as a physician in nearby Heidingsfeld upon graduating, he entered the Dutch army. This remarkable career move came about as a result of Siebold's close acquaintance with François Joseph Harbaur (1776–1824), a fatherless refugee from Alsace, who had been taken in by Siebold's father and also studied medicine in Würzburg. Twenty years Siebold's senior, Harbaur's medical genius had paved the way to a stellar career that brought him into contact with the great names of European enlightenment, including Friedrich Schiller and Johann Wolfgang von Goethe. It eventually earned him the position of personal physician to King Willem I of The Netherlands, and it was in that position that Harbour (who had also become the Dutch military's medical

Heidingsfeld

inspector general) offered Siebold the position of physician-major in the Dutch East Indian Army.

Thus it was that, in the summer of 1822, the twenty-six-year-young German physician, eager to make his mark in the world of science and determined 'to do honor to the name of Siebold,' boarded the Dutch frigate *Adriana* to sail for Batavia. Already on his way there, he began collecting specimens of marine fauna, using the long hours in between to gain a grounding in Malay. But when he arrived in Batavia the next spring, he was struck down by a tropical illness. To recover, he was offered a room at the residence of Governor-General Baron Godert van der Kapellen (1778–1848). The governor-general, who had also studied in Germany, soon took a liking to the German scholar. He was also impressed with Siebold's erudition and, eager to reassert his country's standing in East Asia following the return of the colonies to the Dutch in the wake of the Anglo-Dutch treaty of 1814, he decided to dispatch Siebold to Japan. The German, who had very much set his eyes on the Dutch East Indies, was willing enough to play his part in the promotion of Western science but already knew enough about Japan to realize that the country for which he was now bound would present a challenge to his own ambitions to explore and discover:

> Unexpectedly, I saw myself removed from these prospects. The goal, which I had set myself on my journey to the East Indies, and which I had managed to gradually bring closer, was now about to be readjusted toward a country so peculiar, so far removed from Europe. Not to a country, moreover, where men live in freedom—no, to a nation where the shrewd powers that be prevent one from all free traffic with the country and its people!

Yet adjust his goal Siebold did. And he did so in a most remarkable fashion. Instead of Malay, he now applied himself to the Japanese language and its difficult writing system with thousands of Chinese characters. He already spoke Dutch and it was through this language, the *lingua franca* among Japanese intellectuals and scientists, that he began to teach the local *rangakusha*, the 'scholars of Dutch' in the fields of medicine and natural sciences upon his arrival in Nagasaki in August 1823. Aware of the German's contribution, the authorities turned a blind eye to Siebold's comings and goings, so much so that, while his Dutch employers remained confined on their island, Siebold was allowed to go ashore. With time, he spent more time on the shore than on the island, much of it at his Narutaki-*juku*, a small

*Siebold's Narutaki-*juku *near Nagasaki*

school that stood on Nagasaki's eastern outskirts. The Japanese, too, recognized the German's genius, and before long, his school became a place of pilgrimage for leading scholars from all over Japan, among them Takano Chōei, Itō Genboku, Itō Keisuke, Koseki Sanei, and Ninomiya Keisaku. All of these men went on to make important contributions to Japan's scientific development, though not all were rewarded for their services, especially those who ventured outside their fields of expertise and into the realm of politics. Thus Takano Chōei would spend five years in prison for criticizing the Tokugawa authorities for opening fire on the American merchant vessel *Morrison*. Watanabe Kazan, who did not study at the Narutaki-*juku* but did meet Siebold in Edo, was also imprisoned for his pro-Western stance. Hearing of Chōei and Kazan's plight, their fellow-scholar Koseki Sanei committed *seppuku* shortly afterward.

Siebold, too, would eventually run foul of the Japanese authorities, but only at the very end of his five-year stay. During that time, he amassed a huge collection of household goods, tools, hand-crafted objects, woodprints, down to stuffed animals, and plant species. He also took up living with a Japanese woman, not one of the many women of pleasure who daily crossed the bridge to Dejima to keep its occupants company, but the daughter of a Nagasaki merchant. She went by the name of O-Taki and gave birth to a baby daughter, whom they named Ine. Ine, too, would follow in her father's family tradition, becoming the first Japanese woman to be trained as a physician. She began her study under two of Siebold's students, first under Ninomiya Keisaku, who taught her the fundamentals of medicine, then under Ishii Sōken, who taught her obstetrics; and later under Johan Pompe van Meerdervoort (1829–1908), a Dutch physician attached to the Naval Training Center established in Nagasaki with Dutch help in 1855. She went on to have a distinguished career, a career that was crowned when she became the personal physician to the northern *daimyō* Date Munenari.

As with his predecessors, the highlight of Siebold's stay in Japan was his long journey to Edo, some three years into his stay in Japan. The factor of Dejima, at the time, was the freshly appointed Willem de Sturler (1774–1855), a military man who had been wounded whilst campaigning for Willem V. Probably to assist Siebold, Sturler chose to be accompanied not only by his chief physician, but by two more Europeans: Heinrich Bürger, whom Siebold had already met in Batavia in the capacity of druggist and had been sent to Japan to assist Siebold, and a certain Karl Hubert de Villeneuve, an illustrator who would do a number of drawings to accompany Siebold's writings. Being the chief physician, Siebold was still called upon to treat

Sturler at his Dejima residence

Japanese patients along the way, many of whom suffered from chronic, neglected, or incurable afflictions. Feeling indebted to his hosts, Siebold patiently obliged, doing what little he could with the limited resources at his disposal. He did so with a sense of guilt, often coming away with the feeling of 'having to play the charlatan against my will.' It was probably because of this that he never accepted any payments for his medical services, though he did gracefully accept

xlvi

the many gifts from patients of his medical students in Nagasaki, by those he met on his trip to Edo, and from the dignitaries and scholars with whom he met in Osaka, Kyoto, and Edo. And it was one such gift—a collection of detailed maps of Japan and Korea from the hands of cartographer Inō Tadataka (1745–1818), and gifted to him by court astronomer Takahashi Kageyasu (1785–1829)—that eventually landed him in trouble when he was about to sail home in 1828.

Siebold and his wife and child observing the arrival of a Dutch ship

Siebold was set to embark on the *Cornelius Houtman* toward the middle of August. In the weeks leading up to his departure, part of his amassed collection, which by now comprised thousands of items, was carried aboard. But on 10 August disaster struck when the vessel was blown ashore in a typhoon. In an effort to salvage the vessel, the local governor ordered its cargo to be brought ashore, and it was then that one of his officers discovered Tadataka's maps of Japan and

Korea. The authorities weren't amused. They placed Siebold under house arrest. Siebold refused to furnish them with any names but Takahashi Kageyasu nevertheless ended up in prison, where he died soon after. Lengthy negotiations between the Japanese and the Dutch authorities ensued. They lasted until 22 October of the next year, when the *bakufu* banned the German from Japan. Finally, on 2 January 1830, Siebold set sail from Nagasaki aboard the *Java*. His vast collection, however, was spared. Having removed all sensitive materials, the authorities returned it to its owner—all twenty thousand items of specimens of mammals, fish, birds, reptiles, invertebrates, and species of plants.

Siebold's vast collection and the detailed observations he made on his journey to Edo, formed the basis of three major works: the *Fauna Japonica*, published in five volumes in Leiden with the help of naturalists attached to Leiden University as well as those he had trained in Japan; the *Flora Japonica*, published in two volumes in Leiden with the help of the German botanist Joseph Gerhard Zuccarini (1797–1848); and his magnum opus *Nippon: Record with a View of Describing Japon and its Neighboring Islands and Protectorates: Ezo and the Southern Kuril Islands, Karafuto, Korea and the Ryūkyū Islands, based on Japanese and European Writings and my own Observations* (*Nippon: Archiv zur Beschreibung von Japan und dessen Neben- und Schutzländern: Jezo mit den südlichen Kurilen, Krafto, Kooraï und den Liukiu-Inseln, nach japanischen und europäischen Schriften und eigenen Beobachtungen bearbeitet*). It only saw the full light of day in all its glory when, in 1879, the Würzburg publisher Leo Woerl (1845–1918) published it in two volumes under the slightly altered title, *Nippon: Archiv zur Beschreibung von Japan und dessen Neben- und Schutzländern: Jezo mit den südlichen Kurilen, Sachalin, Korea und den Liukiu-Inseln.*

Among those 'European Writings' mentioned in Siebold's initial, self-published work were, of course, the works from Kaempfer's hand. Taken together, the body of work of the two German titans remains the single most important source on Edo period Japan in any Western language. Perhaps it was that typical German aptitude for *gründlichkeit* (thoroughness) that made both men describe their experiences and observations in such all-encompassing granular

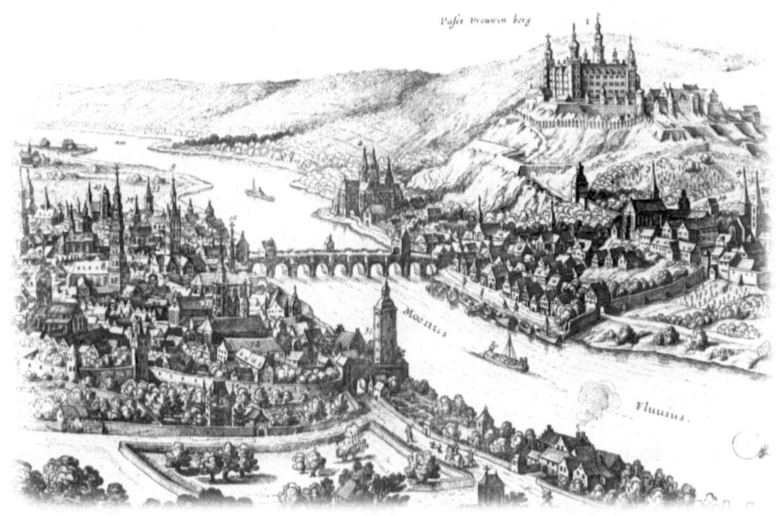

Würzburg

detail. In sheer volume alone, Kaempfer's work clearly comes out as the winner. His two-volume work, spanning a total of 871 folio pages, exceeds that of his fellow countryman, though, at 828 pages, Siebold's work still comes in as close second. Kaempfer's journey to Edo, too, covers more paper, the entire 365 pages of his second volume. Yet this comparison is perhaps also unfair as Kaempfer made two journeys during his stay, whereas Siebold only made one. In

xlix

that light, Siebold's description of his single journey, which covers 232 pages, comes out favorably when compared to Kaempfer's account, especially when one leaves out the latter's fifty-page appendix and Kaempfer's exhaustive description of the Mission's 'preparations for the journey, his 'general description of the way by water and land from Nagasaki to Edo,' the 'post houses, inns, eating houses, and tea houses' that can be found along the way, the 'great number of people who daily travel on the roads', and his view 'of our journey to the Emperor's Court in general,' which together take up another fifty odd pages.

In some respects, Siebold's work can even be considered more thorough—exhausting, rather than exhaustive, even—especially where it concerns his observations on Japan's flora and fauna. It is especially Siebold's fastidiousness in these fields that can make for tedious reading. When, shortly into his journey, he is reminded of Japan's likeness to Europe in its four seasons, he cannot help but enumerate each and every tree and plant that heralds their arrival or departure. And thus, where a few sentences would suffice to paint the picture, he spends four whole pages describing which flower blooms when, which tree sheds its leaves in what month, and when they grow back again—all accompanied by extensive notes with their Latin species names and their Japanese equivalents. The same happens when he describes Japan's heavily cultivated landscape:

A more than a thousand-year-long intercourse with the neighboring Asian mainland, chiefly with China, Korea, and the more southernly situated Ryūkyū Islands, has enriched Japan's flora with many exotic, useful, and decorative plants, and the scene of an inhabited countryside has an unmistakable alien

1

character enhanced through artifice. Where, on the slopes of hills we now see springing forth terrace-like beds with cereals and vegetables, there once proliferated grasses—variants of *Erianthus, Ischaemum, Anthesteria, Cenchrus, Imperata,* and *Andropogon,* entwined with the branches of *Smilax, Dolichos, Celastrus,* the *Clematis, Kadsura* and *Lonicera,* the *Dioscorea* and *Asclepias* species. Where now, tea bushes border fields filled with oilseed rape, tobacco, buckwheat, saffron, poppy, sesame, hemp, and cotton, once waxed a colorful mixture of *Elaeagnus, Viburnum, Spiraca, Hydrangeae, Euryen, Callicarpa, Rhamnus, Rubus, Crataegus, Lespedeza, Lycium,* and *Styrax* species. Where rice now covers hour-long flats with a monotone green, once lay swamps covered with *Nelumbium* and *Euryale, Potamogeton, Pontederia, Alisma, Trapa,* and other *Hydrocharitaceae,* while their solitary banks were lined with reed and sedge species— *Sparganium, Typha, Zizania, Erianthus, Leersia,* and *Kyllinga.* Or rivers and mountain streams still freely widened their beds, their banks bristling with *Bambusa, Ficus, Croton, Boehmeria,* and *Procris.* On their alluvial soils grew *Commelineae, Chenopodium, Polygonoideae, Solanum, Fumariaceae,* and *Ranunculus,* and *Panzeria, Saururus, Veronica, Houttuynia, Hydrocotyle.* And species of *Sedum, Astragalus, Hypericum, Potentilla, Ruellia, Carpesium, Euphorbia, Prenanthes, Artemisia,* and other radiant flowers covered village greens and hills.

OK, we get the picture. For a botanist with a keen interest in Japan's flora, such passages may present a page-turner, but for the average reader with a more general interest in Japan, they can be a bit of a slog. They, too, can't wait to turn the page, but for somewhat different reasons. Yet, then again, Siebold wasn't in the business of writing touristy travel blogs; his and Kaempfer's aim was to further science. And this they did with unrelenting, unswerving, unflinching, uncompromising dedication—you get the picture.

The occasional scientific relapse aside, both Kaempfer's and Siebold's accounts of the Mission's journey to Edo and back to Nagasaki are still fascinating to read. It is a journey through a country so far removed from their own that they had to employ al their descriptive skills to make it understandable to their European audiences. The country they described no longer exists. It has been replaced by a country that has proudly taken center stage in a modern world filled with airports, bullet trains, and high-rise buildings. Yet even now, hidden away among the clutter of this advanced, high-tech conundrum of a country, we can still find traces of a realm still fully in tune with its age-old traditions, a countryside that still casts a spell on those who pass through it, populated by a people who live in harmony with their surroundings.

Prologue

Looking down from my port-side window on a domestic night flight from Tokyo to Nagasaki, the Japanese isles below looked like a fairy-tale landscape, a tapestry of little lights of various shades and colors, some moving some stationary, some blinking some static, weaving a web-like fabric spun over a thousand miles.

Reality, of course, was somewhat different. I knew that large swathes of the light-studded carpet sliding away underneath me were industrial areas: oil refineries, shipbuilding yards, car plants, chemical plants, power stations, heavy industries—a highly urbanized belt stretching from Tokyo to Hiroshima. The resulting fumes are allegedly one of the reasons why most Japanese still hide their faces behind a pre-shaped mixture of paper, plastic, and cotton wool. Whereas the rest of the world has largely cast aside this nuisance, the Japanese are doggedly persevering in wearing their beloved face masks. Even after the World Health Organization declared the pandemic over, the Japanese authorities could not bring themselves to tell its people to call it a day. They must have realized the indispensable role the throw-away surgical mask has come to play since its invention more than half a century ago. Apart from the poor air quality in industrialized areas, an often cited reason is that in such a densely populated country it is a good way to prevent local outbreaks of flu from turning into full-blown epidemics. And, true enough, many a Japanese who is caught sniveling feels obliged to cover his or her face with masks that seem to have grown with each decade so that, by now, just the eyes are exposed.

But in Japan, the mask works in more subtle ways too. Many Japanese don a mask, even when they are perfectly healthy, thus signaling to those around them (especially to their colleagues at work), look at me! Look to what extraordinary lengths I go to safeguard your precious health. The mask also has a more negative use, when its wearer rather wouldn't be seen. On the innocent side of the scale are women who want to hide the fact they aren't using any makeup. More sinister are those who try to hide away altogether, withdrawing to the warm and moist comfort of their shrinking world, preferring to inhale their own stale breath over a breath of fresh air.

The Pandemic, of course, only served to reinforce these deeply entrenched proclivities. Judging by the crowds on Tokyo's busy streets, it fixed them for eternity.

Where the Pandemic had a devastating impact on the country's economy, the attending masks lent it a modest boost. Thus, while in 2012, the domestic production of masks still hovered at 2.8 billion, in 2021—at the height of the Pandemic—it soared to 16.3. Already in 2018, the total sales of disposable face masks in Japan amounted to ¥36 billion (roughly $250 million). And when, early on in the pandemic, the government issued an advice to wear a mask at all times, all face masks made of high-tech breathable fabric were sold out the moment they went on sale.

The abiding popularity of face masks has also spawned a new industry that promotes the mask as a new fashion assessory. Some come with small pockets into which their wearer can insert ice packs to cool them down in Japan's hot summers. For those who also want to look smart, there are masks in different colors, printed in a wide array of patterns, and adorned with miniature bow-tied ribbons. Some specially shaped and shaded masks are designed to make their wearer look slimmer. This, in turn, has led to contests to decide which wearer deserves the epitaph *masuku bijin,* or 'mask beauty.'

In a culture obsessed with cleanliness, participants in Shintō rituals already covered their mouths with the leaves of the *sakaki,* the sacred Shintō tree, during the Heian period (794–1185). It is a tradition that is still observed at Kyoto's Yasaka Shrine and Osaka's Otori Shrine. Yet it was another lethal pandemic, the Spanish flu in the wake of WWI, that made the face mask a regular feature in Japanese public life. Since then, the mask has only gained in popularity, so that even now, at least seven out of ten Japanese continue to wear a mask when they go out of doors. Indeed, some wearers have become so attuned to their second face that they have lost the capacity to smile. A whole new profession of dedicated 'smile coaches,' now help sufferers to retrain their atrophied facial muscles—'say "*ri*"' (the equivalent of 'say "cheese"')—to produce an expression faintly approaching bliss.

It will take much more, then, than a piece of fatherly advice to make the Japanese shake their addiction to wearing masks. And thus, while the authorities have formally opened Japan up again for tourists, declaring all but the Fukushima area safe for travel, they have wisely refrained from telling their people to tone it down a little with the masks.

To accommodate this national fetishism, the cabin crew of the Air France flight into Tokyo generously supplied all passengers with a *kit sanitaire.* As the airplane docked, and we foreign passengers hesitantly followed the brave example of the native passengers stepping into the gangway, it felt as if we were entering a giant operating theater—a theater whose protagonists must be protected from all the germs and viruses lurking in a dangerous outside world.

The question for me—an outside person—was whether I would be able to enter this theater and get a glimpse of what was behind the mask. Moreover, would I be able to partly lift the veil cast by centuries of modernization to reveal the contours of an older Japan, a country perhaps more quintessentially Japanese? A Japan that had closed itself off from the outside world during two-and-a-half centuries of splendid isolation. A Japan only a handful of men attached to the Dutch Missions had seen.

Nagasaki Kaidō

The Nagasaki Kaidō, was the first leg of the Mission's journey to Edo. It ran from the port of Nagasaki to the port of Kokura. Kokura, in turn, lay on the Strait of Shimonoseki, the channel that separates Kyushu from the main island of Honshū. The old high road, then, not only connected Nagasaki to the island of Honshū but also, by way of the strait, to the maritime traffic arteries of Japan's Inland Sea and west coast.

The Nagasaki Kaidō has a history that precedes written records. The route, which covers mainly flat terrain and crosses only one serious pass, has probably been walked since the Japanese Isles were first inhabited. Its importance grew during the Asuka period (538–710), when the imperial court at Asuka (not far from Nara) established regional offices at Dazaifu (just east of present-day Fukuoka). Yet it was the development of Nagasaki as the island's first foreign port of call during the early Edo period that really put the high road on the map. The bakufu *government in Edo (Tokyo) decided to make it into a proper* kaidō, *a kind of national high road, though still managed and maintained by the domains through which it passed. Like Japan's other main traffic arteries, the Nagasaki Kaidō had a large number of* shukuba *or 'post towns,' some twenty-three by the end of the 17th century. It stretched for fifty-seven* ri *(roughly 140 miles) and took the average traveler a week to complete.*

Though the port of Nagasaki lent the high road its official name, it was also known as the Sato no Michi, or the Sugar Road. As the name suggests, the main commodity transported along the high road was sugar, which was imported to Japan from mainland China. At first, it reached Nagasaki in

Chinese junks; later it became an important and often overlooked part of the nanban bōeki, *the 'barbarian trade' with the Portuguese and the Dutch.*

The southern part of the Nagasaki Kaidō largely followed one of two routes. One leg set out from Nagasaki, turned west and followed the eastern shore of Ōmura Bay until it reached the port of Sonogi. From there, the road turned inland toward Ureshino. The other leg crossed the isthmus between Ōmura Bay and the Ariake Sea, following its western shore until the two roads joined each other again at the castle town of Saga. The Dutch Missions usually took the western route and, if weather allowed, a shortcut across Ōmura Bay from Tokitsu to Sonogi.

Dejima

Of course I had to start my journey on Dejima, the small fan-shaped island at the foot of Nagasaki Bay. At the time of its construction, it was the farthest point to which Nagasaki extended into the bay. Today, the city has caught up with the island. It has encroached on the bay by another five hundred yards so that the Nagasaki Seaside Park now takes pride of place in overlooking the bay.

The tour guide for the day was Takahashi-*san*, a dapper octogenarian dressed up like a true Edo-period official. He wore a samurai's *hakama* and a long sword tucked into his belt. Since the island was wholly manmade, he explained, it was at first known as Shikijima or Artificial Island. But since it was a place of coming and going, the name Dejima, or 'Departure Island' won out. Various theories exist to explain the island's fan shape. One holds that, asked by his architects what shape it should take, *shōgun* Tokugawa Iemutsu flicked open his fan and said 'make it so.' Another holds that the beachhead at the mouth of the Nakajima River already had a curved shape. The most plausible explanation can be found in Japan's seaside castles, where curved walls have proven the best wave-breakers.

At just 1.5 hectares and densely packed with buildings, the island provided little room for its occupants to go for a stroll. Its main thoroughfare stretches for just two hundred yards. To walk farther one either had to pace it up and down or wait for the annual Edo Sanpu.

Dejima during the late 19th century

None of the buildings that stood on the island during the Edo period have survived. During our hour-long tour, Takahashi-*san* explained how, on 3 April 1798, a huge fire destroyed all the buildings on the island's west wing. The *opperhoofd*'s luxurious quarters, too, were lost. The remainder was dismantled after the Dutch trading post closed in 1859. They had to make room for more modern buildings with double verandas to accommodate foreign settlers and tourists.

The turnaround came in 1951, when Nagasaki City drew up plans to restore the island to its former glory. A year later, it bought up the island. After much pouring over the available data, it decided to restore the island and its structures to the way it had been at the beginning of the 19th century. Work began only in 1996, but in April 2000, just in time for the tourist season, the project was completed. Next, the city rebuilt the 130-yard, sea-facing wall that protected the island's south side. They also rebuilt the Sui-*mon*, the large gate in front of the landing jetty, the *opperhoofd*'s quarters, and a number of other structures. The crowning moment came on 24 November 2017, when in the presence of Dutch royalty, the Omotemon Footbridge reconnected Dejima to the mainland.

If it is up to Nagasaki's town planners, this is just the beginning. A third, even more ambitious plan, envisions Dejima as a proper island again, fully encircled by water. For this to happen, a number of high-rise buildings, as well as the busy three-lane highway (euphemistically called the Dejima Seaside Avenue) that skirts the island on the west side, will have to give way, or at least move a few hundred yards. It is questionable whether, under the present economic circumstances, this plan will ever be realized. But, hey, it is always nice to dream of a better future.

While all the present buildings on the island are replicas, some of the old foundations remain. You can see them through large glass windows set in the floors of a number of buildings that stand on a large concrete frame suspended over the old foundations. The old landing jetty can also be glimpsed in this fashion. Through the thick glass, you can see a wide staircase descending through the island's sea wall toward the water's edge and the moored boats. It was by such small boats that the Dutch carried the cargo of their large merchantmen ashore. There it was carefully weighed, registered, and made ready to begin its journey along the Nagasaki Kaidō.

One other important commodity came ashore here: the latest news. Being the only ones allowed into Japan besides the Chinese, the Dutch were a window to the outside world. The *bakufu* government in Edo highly valued the news they brought about events in Europe. They were even more interested in the Far-East activities of other Western powers—the Portuguese, the Spanish (and later the British, the French, the Germans, and the Russians). Local interpreters meticulously recorded every detail and sent reports to Edo in the form of *fūsetsu-gaki* or 'books of rumors.' That title alone shows the Japanese did not swallow everything the Dutch presented to them as truth.

Departure

On the eve of my departure, I wanted to pay a visit to a local temple. Both Siebold and Fischer mention how, on the morning of their departure, they and the *opperhoofd* paid a visit to a temple to pray for a safe journey. Siebold correctly indicates it as the Ifuku Temple. Fischer incorrectly identifies it as the Tenjin Temple, an error that is explained in passing by Siebold:

> The procession made a halt at the Ifuku Temple, and we, along with our guides, entered one of its halls to pray for the protection of the heavenly spirit Tenjin.

Tenjin, in fact, had once been a mortal being. He was a man known by the name of Sugawara no Michizane (845–903), a poet, scholar, and politician during the Heian period. It was his talent in the field of politics that eventually spelled his downfall. In 901, a clique of court officials conspired against him and persuaded the emperor to relegate him to a petty function at the Dazaifu in Kyushu. There he died, according to some of a broken heart. But Michizane got his revenge. No sooner had he passed away than plague, drought, and famine spread throughout the realm. When storms, lightning, and floods also struck the capital for weeks on end and various members of the imperial family perished, the emperor repented. He posthumously restored Michizane to his former rank and deified him as Tenjin-*sama*, or the Sky Deity. Tenjin-*sama* was especially worshipped in Kyushu, his place of exile, including Nagasaki, where a wandering monk from Karatsu established a small wayside shrine. It became known as the Tenman-*gū*, a name given to many shrines dedicated to Michizane's spirit. The monk's name was Ifuku Kōjun, and when, in 1622, a proper temple replaced the shrine, it was renamed the Ifuku Temple. Situated at the start of the Nagasaki Kaidō, the temple grounds became the place from where the Missions would start out. Nagasaki officials would assemble the long train on its grounds and toast with cups of *sake* with its Dutch members on the eve of their departure.

The Ifuku Temple has long since gone. And so, on the eve of my own departure, I decided to instead pay a visit to the Sōfuku Temple, not because their names are similar but because it was visited by *Opperhoofd* Jan Cock Blomhoff on his departure. The temple was built by another foreign community in Nagasaki: the Chinese. Like the Dutch, they too were allowed to stay on when the Portuguese and Spanish were kicked out. At that time, only a few Chinese traders lived in Nagasaki, for the Ming court forbade its subjects from crossing over to Japan. They were afraid of the *wakō*, the fearsome Japanese pirates, who preyed on shipping in the China Sea.

Things changed in 1684, when the Qing court lifted the ban after the *bakufu* managed to eliminate the *wakō* threat. At that time, the Chinese in Nagasaki still lived alongside the Japanese. To accommodate the new influx of Chinese traders and to prevent smugglers from landing elsewhere, the governor of Nagasaki ordered

Today's main entrance to the Sōfuku Temple

the construction of the Tōjin-*yashiki*, or 'Chinese Mansion.' The term 'mansion' was a bit of a misnomer, really; the Tōjin-*yashiki* was a veritable Chinatown. It had a market, various temples, and a public bathhouse. With a surface area of well over three hectares, it was twice the size of Dejima. At its heyday, it housed a staggering two thousand Chinese. It was located on a square plot of land just southeast of Dejima. Though not an island, it was surrounded by a

11

wall and moat. This did not mean that those who dwelled in the Tōjin-*yashiki* were locked up; unlike the Dutch, the Chinese could freely enter the city, though guards posted at the settlement's main gate watched their every move.

In Sharp contrast to the meticulous care with which Dejima has been restored, hardly a trace remains of the Tōjin-*yashiki*. The reason is that, in 1784, the whole place burned down in a massive fire. Much

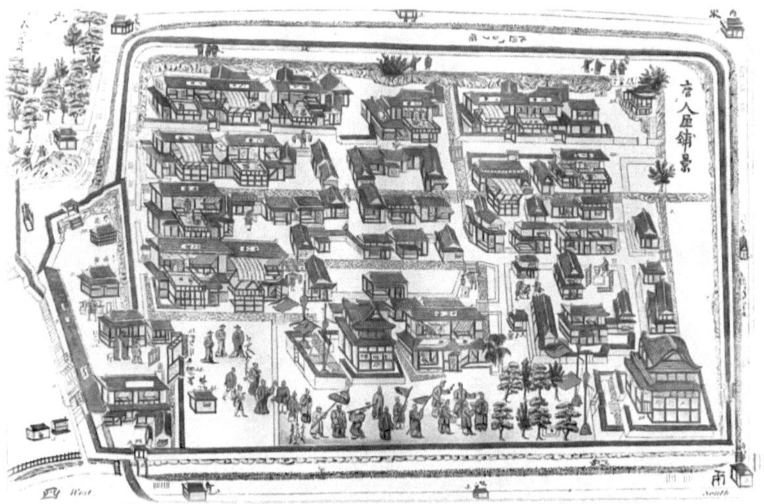

The Tojin Yashiki

of it was rebuilt, but another large conflagration undid all the hard work in 1870. By then, the settlement had largely been abandoned; Nagasaki had been opened to foreign settlers, and the Chinese were no longer required to live within the settlement's confines.

One might be led to believe that Nagasaki's present-day Chinatown was built on the ruins of the Tōjin-*yashiki*, but this would be a mistake. The original settlement was located farther to the southeast,

12

in an area now known as the Kannai Township. Today, just three of the Tōjin-*yashiki*'s former structures remain: the Tojin-*dō*, the Tenko-*dō*, and the Kannon-*dō*. A fourth building, the Fukken Kaikan Hall was built during the Meiji period (1868–1912). The Sōfuku Temple, though not part of the Chinese settlement, is a living reminder of that time, as it was built and frequented by its dwellers.

Walking around the grounds of the Sōfuku Temple, I found the temple exactly as Blomhoff described it two centuries earlier, including a huge cauldron:

> In the said temple stood a cauldron of cast iron, which was five feet high and equally wide. The cauldron is said to be two hundred years old and large enough to feed two thousand people at once. According to legend, the pot was only used once, in a time of war.

A notice in front of the cauldron was more precise:

> In the year 1680 the failed harvest led to a shortage of rice, and people in Nagasaki, too, died of starvation. In order to rescue the starving, Fukusaiji Temple started to hand out cooked rice to the people during the New Year of 1681. The Sōfuku Temple was unable to do the same as it was undergoing reconstruction. So when the work finished, on the first day of the ninth month, the fourth-generation chief priest of Sōfuku Temple, Sengan, went around the town to beg for alms and started offering rice. In February 1682, work was begun on the manufacturing of a cauldron. It was completed on the fourteenth day of the fourth month, and

taken from the Kajiya Township on wheels to the kiln in front
of the main hall at Sōfuku Temple, upon which it was placed.

The cauldron wasn't the only thing that caught Blomhoff's attention:

> At the heart of the temple stood two large statues, some seven
> feet tall and both marvelously crafted, with protruding eyes
> and fearsome faces. These monsters are kept and venerated as
> Sea Gods. Each of them holds in his right hand a long pike.
> One holds his left hand in front of his eyes and can see, it is
> said, as far as a thousand miles.

The demons described by Blomhoff were known by their Chinese
worshippers as Qianliyan, the Thousand-Mile Eye, and Shunfeng'er,
the Wind-Following Ear. Able to discern the most distant threats,
they were the guardians (and lovers) of Mazu, a deity to which the
temple's main hall is dedicated. A notice in front of the hall read:

> Mazu is the goddess of the seas, also known by the names of
> Tianhoushengmu, Tianfei, Laoma, Pusa, and others. She is
> particularly revered in the southern regions of China. Statues
> of the goddess were worshipped before Chinese vessels set out
> to sea, and one of these statues was lowered from a Chinese
> ship while anchored in the port of Nagasaki and enshrined in
> the Chinese-style Mazu Hall at Sōfukuji Temple.

So I had come to the right temple. I too would be boarding
numerous boats on my passage through the Inland Sea. They might

not exactly be Chinese junks, but having paid my respect, I had good hopes Tianhoushengmu would protect me.

The next day was a beautiful spring day, and I got up at the first shimmer of light. The first stretch, a pleasantly narrow road around the southern slope of Hōka-*zan* or Mt. Beacon, led along a string of Buddhist temples: the Shōfuku-*ji*, the Higashi Hongan-*ji*, and the Honren-*ji*.

The huge cauldron on the grounds of the Sōfuku Temple

At no point, even at the temples' elevated position, did I get so much as a glimpse of Nagasaki Bay. That privilege remained to the happy few living atop Nagasaki's tallest high-rise buildings. How different it must have been when Siebold took this road two hundred years ago. He would have been treated to a breathtaking panorama as the long procession slowly turned inland from the bustling port: the curved roofs within the walls of the Chinese settlement toward

15

the east, the Dutch *tricolore* proudly flying over the rows of Dutch buildings on the island at the foot of the bay, and, beyond it, Chinese junks and Dutch merchantmen riding at anchor.

Martyrs

The temples along the first short stretch of the Nagasaki Kaidō were followed by the Twenty-six Martyrs Museum. It was built on the same site where, more than four centuries ago, twenty-six men—seventeen Japanese members of the Third Order of St. Francis, three Japanese Jesuits, four Spaniards, one Portuguese, one Mexican, the latters six all Franciscan missionaries—as well as three altar boys, were crucified on the orders of despot Toyotomi Hideyoshi. Their terrible end came as a direct result of the *San Felipe* Incident.

A year earlier, on 12 July, the Spanish galleon *San Felipe* had set out from Manilla in the Philippines toward Acapulco on the west coast of Mexico. It wasn't a smart move; sailing that late in the season meant it would be crossing the Pacific Ocean when it became the playground of typhoons. And sure enough, just a few hundred miles into its passage the vessel lost most of its sails and rigging, forcing its crew to cut down the main mast to keep the ship from capsizing. Ditching all of the cargo except some 600,000 *pesos*, they finally reached the east coast of the island of Shikoku on 19 October of the same year, 1596.

Chōsokabe Motochika (1539–99), the lord of nearby Kōchi Castle, who commanded a fleet of his own, ordered his captains to tow the Spanish vessel into Urado Bay. The operation did not go according to plan. The vessel next got stuck on a sandbank at the mouth of the

16

bay. Or maybe it did go according to plan, for the vessel was now shipwrecked and, according to Japanese law, the local authorities could impound what remained of the vessel and its cargo. But when Captain Matheus de Randicio protested, Motochika got cold feet. This was, after all, an international affair, so he better contact the authorities in Kyoto. Luckily, he had his connections there, and so he referred the captain to Mashita Nagamori (1545–1615), one of Toyotomi Hideyoshi's five commissioners. Nagamori decided to travel down to Kōchi in person, allegedly to take stock of the situation but furtively so he could extort a bribe to cover his 'expenses.' Again, the ship's captain protested, and thus Nagamori had no other choice than to confiscate its precious cargo on behalf of Hideyoshi and send it to Kyoto.

While the 600,000 *pesos* were being transferred to smaller vessels, Nagamori used his time to make a register, not only of the vessel's cargo but also of its crew. Whether Spanish or black slaves, all were detained within the castle town and forced to surrender their personal possessions. Next, he proceeded to 'interview' them, according to the Spanish while they entertained him with music, games, and a demonstration of European fencing techniques.

A particularly telling interview was the one with the vessel's pilot, Francisco de Olandia (judging by his surname a Dutchman). The pilot angrily grabbed back one of the confiscated maps, rolled it out, and pointed out to the Japanese official just how tiny Japan was in comparison to Spain and its overseas possessions. Asked by Nagamori how Spain had managed to acquire such vast possessions, the pilot conceded that the King of Spain first sent in missionaries, shortly followed by conquistadors so that, having been converted to the Christian faith, the locals could be subdued all the more readily.

Whatever the exact conditions under which the prisoners surrendered their information, the impression Nagamori came away with did not produce a very flattering view of Spanish activities in the Pacific. In a long letter to Hideyoshi in Kyoto, he concluded that:

> The Spanish are pirates, and there is no doubt that they have come to Japan with a design to make it submit to their will by military force, as they have done in Peru and Mexico. This is what I have also been told by three Portuguese, as well as others in Kyoto.

Hideyoshi's response was predictable. Though happy with the Iberians' Western arms, he hadn't been too pleased with their proselytizing. Already a decade earlier, on 4 July 1587, he had issued an ordinance forbidding Christian *daimyō* to convert their subjects by force, to sell Japanese subjects to the Iberians to serve as slaves in their empires, or to eat horse and cow meat. Not a word, however, about the missionaries themselves. Just how volatile his stance toward them already was at that stage was revealed by a second, radically different ordinance, issued only a day later. 'Since Japan is a country of the gods,' it stated, 'it is unnatural to introduce heretical teachings from Christian countries.' The Iberian missionaries were no longer welcome, and had to 'make ready to leave Japan within twenty days.' With their profitable trade in mind, he had stopped short of expelling all Iberians, as long as their activities did not 'interfere with the Buddhist faith.'

Upon receipt of Nagamori's report, Hideyoshi immediately reissued his ban on Christianity and ordered all missionaries in the capital to be apprehended forthwith. All were condemned to death. Their sentence was to be carried out at the foot of Nagasaki Bay, to serve as a reminder to all foreigners who put into port with a view to proselytize. And so it happened. On 5 February 1597, on the western slope of a cold and windswept Nishizaka Hill, twenty-six hapless men and boys were crucified. It was done in the Japanese manner, tied to double crosses, their guts and heart pierced by long lances. Their end came only after they had been tortured, mutilated, and paraded through the streets of every city, town, village, and hamlet,

The twenty-six martyrs are crucified at Nishizaka Hill

all the way from Kyoto to Nagasaki. After such an ordeal their deaths must have come as a relief.

Thought they might have raised an eyebrow, the Dutch on nearby Dejima can't have been too unhappy about the whole episode. After all, the persecution of the foreign missionaries led to the eventual departure of the Iberians, giving the Dutch a monopoly on Western trade with Japan. The English, too, had left. They weren't forced;

19

they simply didn't have the stomach to swallow the increasingly restrictive conditions under which they were allowed to trade. In 1623 the East India Company reluctantly closed its factory in Hirado without ever having made a profit.

The Dutch, on their side, had no problem with the Japanese demands. They were there for the lucrative trade in silk, silver, and gold, not to win souls. Being Protestant, they also had no qualms with spitting or trampling on the proffered *fumie*, or 'step-on pictures.' These were also on display at the museum, small plaques with depictions of Jesus and the Holy Mary. Any foreigner willing to desecrate a *fumie* was considered 'sincere' in his loyalty to Japan.

The whole episode put me in mind how, in the wake of Russia's brutal invasion of Ukraine and the decision of foreign multinationals to withdraw their businesses from Russia, the beer giant Heineken went for gold. With typical Dutch opportunism they not only decided to stay on. Oh no, they launched new products to fill the emerging gaps in the local demand for Coke and other soft drinks. We were there to make money, not for political reasons. I was beginning to understand why their beer had always tasted like piss to me.

I reached the museum well before opening time (9:00), but I decided to wait. I wanted to pay my respects. I could use the time to eat some sandwiches from the nearby 7-Eleven. While I admired the museum's Gaudi-like spires, I made notes on my phone and enjoyed the company of some of stray cats in the small park in front of the museum.

Walking along the exhibits in the museum a little later, I (a Dutchman) was struck by the lengths to which the missionaries had gone to spread their faith to the remotest corners of the globe. I was moved by the depth of their conviction, even of the three choir boys.

Thomas, a native of Nagasaki and just thirteen years old, refused to apostatize, professing his undying faith in a last tearful letter to his mother. Thirteen-year-old Anthony, too, refused to abandon his faith. He died singing hymns to his Lord while his mother looked on from nearby. So did twelve-year-old Louis Ibaraki, who continued to sing praise to his Creator even when henchmen cut off one of his ears.

The best-known among the martyrs was a man by the name of Miki Handayū. The son of a samurai, he entered the Society of Jesus in 1585 and became one of its best preachers, earning him the name of Paul Miki. During his own Road to Calvary, being marched to Nagasaki in the midst of winter, he used each stop along the way to spread his message. He did so often in the face of public ridicule and abuse. His last sermon he delivered from the cross, his words recorded by his fellow missionary Luis Frois:

> At this critical time, when you can rest assured that I would not seek to lead you astray, I want to impress on you that man can find no salvation but through Christ. Christ teaches us to forgive our enemies and those who have wronged us. And so I forgive Taikō-*sama* Hideyoshi.

Perhaps the most evocative artifact on display was a tiny crucifix. Delicately carved out of hardwood, its limbs were broken, symbolizing the suffering of Japan's Christian community throughout the ages.

I wondered whether the Japanese had built the museum out of mere historical interest or a sense of guilt—perhaps both? Despite the Tokugawa *bakufu*'s best attempts, there is still a large and thriving Christian community in Kyushu. I remember watching Martin

Scorsese's magisterial *Silence* during my previous flight to Japan. Even the small screen and shitty headphones did not reduce the impact of that harrowing scene in which three Japanese martyrs are crucified along the shore amid the billowing waves of a rising tide. Was it the same fortitude of today's Christian Catholic community that had made the authorities own up to this dark episode and establish this museum and the nearby monument to the memory of their heroes?

Reliquary containing the remains of Paul Miki, Jacob Kisai, and John Goto

Heroes they certainly were, and not unsung. Like tangible messages of faith, their scattered limbs—it was customary for executioners to test their swords on the remains—were secretly preserved by their followers and sent around the world to be venerated as relics. In 1870, French missionaries returned a reliquary containing tiny bone scrapings belonging to Paul Miki and two other martyrs to Nagasaki. By then, their one-time owners had entered the pantheon of Catholic saints. In 1627, Pope Urban III beatified Miki and his fellow martyrs. In 1862 Pope Pius IX canonized all twenty-six of them. They are still listed on the Catholic calendar as San Paolo Miki e Compagni. In 1981, Pope John Paul II visited Nishisaka Hill in person. More recently, Pope Francis did the same. As did John Paul II, who paid homage to the martyrs with the following words:

> Today, I want to be one of the many pilgrims who come to the Martyr's Hill here in Nagasaki, to the place where Christians sealed their fidelity to Christ with the sacrifice of their lives. They triumphed over death in one unsurpassable act of praise to the Lord. In prayerful reflection before the Martyrs' monument, I want to penetrate the mystery of their lives, to let them speak to me and to the whole Church, and to listen to their message which is still alive after hundreds of years.

The Bomb

It was going to be a tough morning, not physically (the road was flat) but emotionally. Less than two miles down the road from the Martyr Museum stood the Nagasaki Atomic Bomb Museum. I knew it had nothing to do with the subject of my journey, except that it may have charred some of the buildings on Dejima Island. But as a Westerner, I could not simply walk by as if nothing had happened.

Occupying a subterranean space under a huge glass dome, the exhibition's opening artifact was a grotesquely deformed grandfather clock. Its hands were frozen at 11:02, the time of detonation. A constant reminder during the first section of the exhibition was the ticking of a clock, ready to stop at the time of impact. A series of video screens displayed image after image of the horrible devastation wrought by the huge fireball and the ensuing pressure blast: contorted metal structures scattered among countless lifeless bodies, toppled gravestones, burned-out cars, and molten roof tiles.

Like Hiroshima, Nagasaki was considered a legitimate target by the Americans. It was one of Japan's major ports and the location of

The clock at the entrance to the exhibition, frozen at the time of impact

a large Mitsubishi shipyard and various other military plants, among them an arms plant and a steel plant. Despite this, it was only a secondary target; the main target had been Kokura, part of today's Kita Kyushu. Major Charles W. Sweeney, the commander of the B-29 Superfortress *Bockscar* had instructions to drop the bomb over Kokura's Yahata Steel Works. Only in case of poor visibility was he to divert his plane to Nagasaki. *Bockscar* arrived over Kokura more than thirty minutes late because of a botched rendezvous with one of the four other planes engaged in the operation. To make matters worse, she also had a failing fuel transfer pump, which shortened her flight time. Sweeney, then, was under considerable pressure to let his bomb go and head back to base. But a cloudy sky, exacerbated by smoke from firebombing the previous day, left him no choice but to fly on to Nagasaki.

They reached the skies above Nagasaki just before eleven, only to find that here, too, heavy clouds obstructed the view. But then, at 11:01, a sudden break in the clouds enabled the bombardier, Kermit Beagan, (yes, that was his real name—I just could not help envisioning two green puppet–like arms operating bomb hatch levers) to sight his target.

Of Nagasaki's population of 2.4 million, 149,266 would perish. A large number of them were incinerated in the fireball that struck those at its epicenter. Many more succumbed to radiation sickness over the next days, weeks, and months. The deaths from leukemia and other forms of cancer spiked in 1951, six years after their sufferers had been exposed to the radiation.

For the remaining five miles of the road to Tokitsu, I was haunted by the images I had seen at the museum. The boy with his whole back stripped bare of skin, lying quivering on his belly as nurses gingerly daubed the oozing mass of red tissue with pieces of gauze. Or the young mother suckling her dying baby. Too weak to suck the milk from her breasts it had died a week later.

I was quietly grateful I had not experienced the kind of reproachful encounter suffered by Alan Booth on his visit to Hiroshima's Peace Memorial Park. But then again, that had been during the nineteen eighties when many of the victims were still alive. Most of the visitors who had visited the museum with me that morning would, like me, have been born after the war.

The nice little village road that had started out along the temples gradually widened until, just at the height of the Twenty-six Martyrs Museum, it merged with the busy New Urakami Road. After that, there was precious little along the road to take my mind off things. Three centuries earlier, Kaempfer came to pretty much the same conclusion:

> Scarce anything remarkable occurred between Nagasaki and Tokitsu. However, to omit nothing, I must take notice, that coming out of Nagasaki we saw the idol of *Jizō*, who is the God of the roads and protector of travelers, hewn out of the rock in nine different places. Another of the same sort stood not far from the village of Urakami, being about three feet long, adorned with flowers and *hana shikimi* [star anise], and placed upon a fathom-high stone pillar. Two other smaller stone pillars, hollow at the top, stood before the idol. Upon these were placed lamps, which travelers light in honor of this idol. At some small distance stood a basin full of water, for those to wash their hands, who had a mind to light the lamps, or to offer anything to the idol.

With most of the hillsides plastered in concrete, there was little chance of me coming across a *jizō* hewn out of the rock face. What did remain was the Tsugiishi Bōzu, a tower of stone naturally shaped into a human figure by the elements over thousands of years. The animistic medieval Japanese, to whom the strangely shaped rock took on a spiritual significance, called it the Stone-stacked Priest.

The Tsuguishi Bōzu

Ōmura Bay

The trip across Ōmura Bay made me quickly forget the horrors of the Atomic Bomb Museum and the endless concrete and tarmac on the road from Nagasaki to Tokitsu. Together with a few other passengers, I boarded the small hydrofoil by which regular service is maintained between Tokitsu and Nagasaki Airport. It should really be named Ōmura Airport as it lies in front of Ōmura City in Ōmura Bay.

Crossing the bay from Tokitsu to Sonogi presented a shortcut in the Nagasaki Kaidō, and it seems that (though Blomhoff and his party skirted the bay via Isahaya) on most occasions the Missions took the shortcut over water. The boats were provided by the lord of Ōmura, who commanded a large fleet to protect his bay-side stronghold of Kushima Castle. Kaempfer, too, crossed the bay in this fashion:

> At Tokitsu we were met by the steward of the household of the Lord of Ōmura, who in the name of his master offered us, out of respect for the *shōgun* and without any consideration, all possible assistance to forward our journey, and acquainted us, at the same time that two *bezaisen*, or pleasure-boats, lay ready to carry us over to Sonogi, which is seven miles and a half distant from Tokitsu. These pleasure boats were built of wood, after the fashion of the country, strong but neat. They were rowed each by fourteen watermen, clad in blue gowns with white lines running across. The prince's flag stood upon the stern, with his coat of arms, being a rose of five leaves in a blue field. Before the flag was placed the usual badge of superior authority, being a bunch of cut paper tied to the end of a long staff, next to which the *bugyō* [magistrate] planted

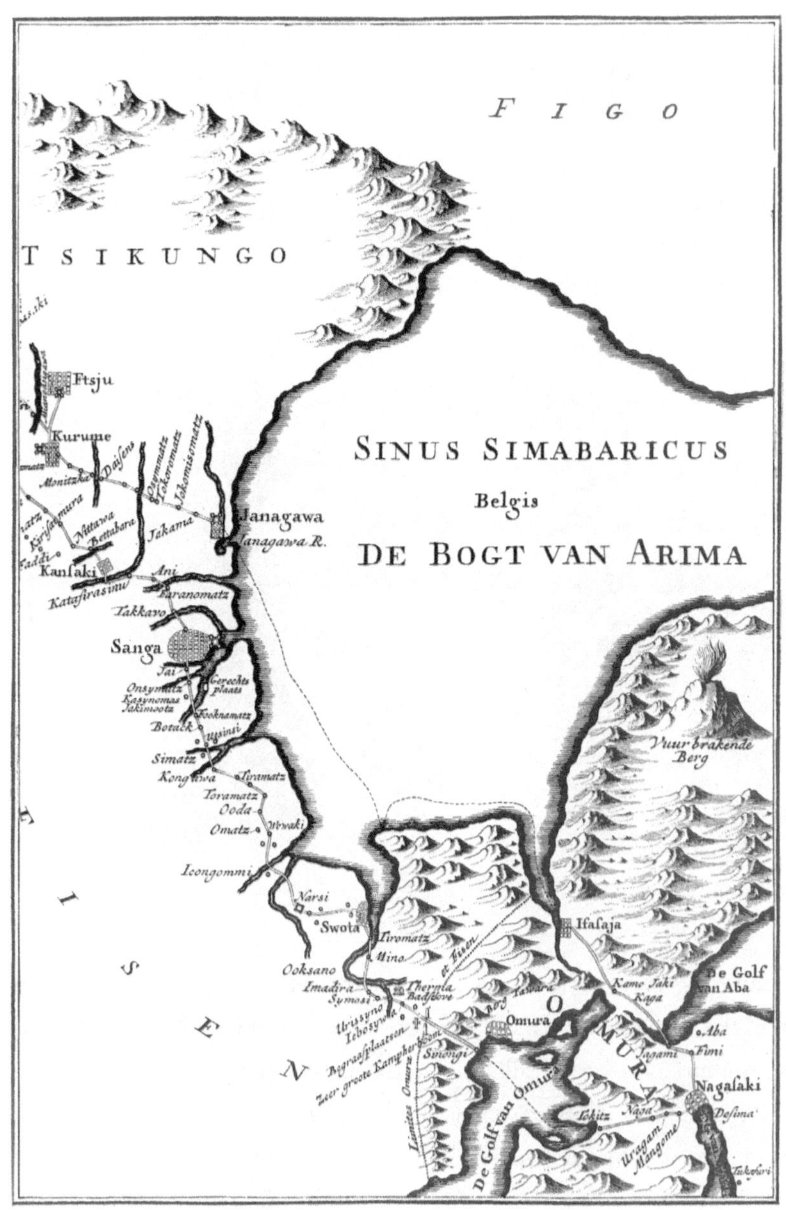

The route of the Dutch Mission from Nagasaki to Kurume

his pike, and then one of the prince's clerks seated himself on one, and the pilot on the other side. The *bugyō* and our resident took possession of the two cabins.

Skimming over the bay's shallow waves at a speed of twenty knots aboard the *Eapootu Rainaa 10*, I could just imagine the sense of freedom the Dutch—a seafaring people—must have felt after their

Ōmura Bay

year-long incarceration on Dejima. It was a wonderful spring day and the surface of the bay's blue ocean water sparkled like diamonds as the emerald-green hills in the distance slid by.

I walked into Ōmura across the long bridge from the airport and understood why the Mission had sailed straight on to Sonogi instead of Ōmura: the city was a disappointment. The only place worth visiting was the Ōmura Historical Park, on the south side of town.

30

It was not much of a park, really, as it had to accommodate an athletic field, a baseball field, an athletic track, as well as lots of parking space for the city's town hall and educational center.

The park's historic reputation had to be upheld by the ruined remains of what was once Kushima Castle. This it did with aplomb. The bayside stronghold was built by Ōmura Yoshiaki (1568–1615), a Christian *daimyō* who had helped Hideyoshi pacify the island of Kyushu during the 1580s. The castle was enlarged during the second decade of the 17th century. Toward the end of the same century, a harbor with boathouses was built to accommodate the domain's large fleet of ships. For the next two centuries the castle stood unchanged, until the Meiji period when, along with so many other beautiful castles, it was largely dismantled. The harbor is still there, along with the restored wall of the inner citadel and a section of the second bailey's southern wall. To top it all, the wall is graced by the Itajiki-*yagura*, the castle's one surviving turret.

Sonogi

The next day, I slept in at Ōmura's drab business hotel on purpose. I wanted to visit Sonogi's local history museum, which only opened at nine. Yet when I arrived at the museum, situated next to a *kofun*, an ancient 'burial mound,' a notice behind the glass entrance doors declared the museum closed for the day.

I sat down on the wooden bench at the entrance to consider my options when presently a young man exited the museum carrying a kettle. Noticing me, he apologized that the museum was closed and asked me where I was from. I told him I had come all the way from Holland to visit his museum only to find it closed. This made him so uncomfortable that I immediately regretted my little lie. But when he asked me to come in anyway, I leaped at the occasion. How could I turn down such an offer? Sonogi's Local History and Folk Artifacts Museum might be small, but no museum proprietor had ever opened his museum just for me.

As we entered the small museum, Izuka-*san* told me there would be an important tea ceremony later that day. And could you believe it? One of the guests would be a Dutch lady from Utrecht! He asked me whether I wanted to attend, but I politely declined. I still had to walk at least ten miles to Ureshino. I also knew from experience that if I sat on my haunches through a whole tea ceremony, I would be close to paraplegic for at least a day.

The museum had little to say about the Edo Sanpu, except that Sonogi was an important post town along the Nagasaki Kaidō. And why should it? The Dutch only stayed at Sonogi for the night. Their passing through must have meant little to the people of Sonogi in historical terms, even while it presented quite a spectacle for the locals. So much, at least, is borne out by the encounter between Fischer and one of Sonogi's elderly occupants:

We went for a stroll outside Sonogi and made a stop at the hovel of an old man who had enjoyed the passage of the Dutch from the days he had been a young boy. He was almost a hundred years old and lived there with a large number of his descendants. More than forty times he had seen our train pass through, and he seemed truly pleased to witness it again. The *opperhoofd* gave him some drinking money so he could treat his family.

Far more important to Sonogi's history, as borne out by the museum's permanent exhibition, was its whaling tradition. Not so much the hunting of whales, Izuka-*san* explained, but the processing of their meat. Situated on the bay and along the Nagasaki Kaidō, Sonogi had developed into a center for whale meat, which was distributed throughout the island and beyond. It still was; walking into town I had seen a number of fishmongers advertising whale meat.

Sonogi's onetime landing place

As I left and thanked Izuka-*san*, he suggested I pay a visit to the town's harbor. It had changed little, he said, since the Missions had passed through. And indeed, the local river wasn't clad in concrete. Instead, its banks were covered in verdant Japanese knotweed. At the end of the river's north bank, just where it poured into the bay, the old landing site seemed untouched by time. It was still graced by a few withering pines and lined with a pebble beach.

Todoroki Falls

The winding road through the hills from Sonogi toward Ureshino was a pleasant change to the mind-numbing monotony of the road from Nagasaki to Tokitsu. The impressions I got couldn't have been that different from the men in whose footsteps I was treading, as most of the route was free of the usual clutter. Two centuries earlier, the Dutch *Opperhoofd* Jan Cock Blomhoff had deigned to alight from his palanquin to see the surrounding from close up. Still writing about himself in the third person, he noted how:

> Most villages are surrounded by firs to such a degree that one would almost mistake them for woods. In passing, Blomhoff, enticed by the weather, would occasionally walk two or three miles in succession and beheld on such occasions things that were most remarkable. On the 15th of February, he perambulated the environs of Ureshino, a very small village. These environs are very famous for their tea, which is dispatched from there in great quantities.

I, too, enjoyed perambulating through these valleys, whose slopes were still covered in tea bushes. I watched as one hill appeared after the other and, with a spring in my step, I followed the road that gradually ascended toward Ureshino.

On my way into Ureshino, I stopped at the Todoroki no Taki, or the Thundering Falls. The falls are among the largest on the island of Kyushu. They are already mentioned in the *Hizen no kuni-fudoki*, a description of Hizen Province recorded in the 6th century. I had been looking forward to staying in Ureshino, for the mountain retreat is also known for its many *onsen*, or 'hot springs.' Already in Kaenpfer's time, it was a popular spa resort and he describes it in great detail:

> Not far from the village, on the side of a small river, which falls down from a neighboring hill, is a hot bath, famous for its virtues in curing the pox, itch, rheumatism, lameness, and several other chronic and inveterate distempers. This bath we had leave to see. I found the place railed in with bamboo in a very handsome manner. Within the inclosure was a watch house, and a small booth for the guests to divert themselves. Along one side of the rails was built a long room or gallery, divided into six smaller rooms, or baths, all under one roof. Every bath was a mat long and broad, and had two cocks, one to let in cold, the other hot water, and this in order that everybody might mix it to what degree of heat they can best bear. At the side of this long room was a place for the guests to repose themselves, covered with a thatched roof. The well was likewise covered with a small square thatched roof. It is not very deep, but the water bubbles out with great vehemence and noise, and is withal so hot, that none of our retinue had courage enough to dip his fingers into it.

Not me! After the long and hot ascent from Sonogi I had plenty of courage to immerse myself in one of its hot springs. I couldn't wait to check in and go look for a nice *onsen*.

The Sansui Global Inn was the only affordable place in town. I was struck by how empty it looked: an empty reception hall, an empty reception counter, and a large but empty glass showcase. Except for two men hunched over a table in the foyer talking in hushed tones, there was no one in sight. I waited a while for someone to appear but no one did. At length, there being not even a bell on the counter to ring, I called out '*Sumimaseen!*.'

'*Haaai,*' a female voice from the rear replied. Presently a young woman appeared. 'Do you have any rooms available,' I asked. At which she said, 'Sorry, but we're out of business.'

The Todoroki Falls

So much for having a nice and well-deserved soak in a local hot spring. It was beginning to dawn on me that the coronavirus pandemic had left its scars on Japan's hospitality trade, too. Numerous affordable hostels I had researched in advance had gone out of business, especially those away from the big cities. Sometimes they still had their signpost, sometimes they carried a notice 'tenant sought,' sometimes they had been replaced by new enterprises.

On my way out of Ureshino, I dropped in at a bookshop situated along the Nagasaki Kaidō. Surely they would have some literature on the old high road. Roused from behind his computer screen, the owner looked startled. He thought long and hard, only to come to the conclusion, '*Aaah, nai desu nee* (Hmmm, sorry but no).' I was quite startled myself. They had plenty of porn *manga* to cater to a traveler's baser needs. But not one little book on the Nagasaki Kaidō?

The youth hostel atop a hill near the next spa town of Takeo also looked abandoned. I rattled the door but it was shut. The hostel too had gone out of business. And so I had to spend a second night in a business hotel. By way of consolation, it had a wonderfully large *furoba*, or 'bathhouse.' I was beginning to fear that business hotels—the least traditional way to spend the night in Japan—might become a standard feature of my trip. It wasn't something I was looking forward to.

Saga

The local history museum in Saga was conveniently situated within the grounds of Saga Castle. So was a large part of the city, for little is left of the former castle buildings that once crowded its wide baileys. Yet even though the city has undergone profound changes since Kaempfer passed through, his description still rang true:

> This city is very large, but extends more in length than in breadth. It is exceedingly populous. Both going in and coming out, we found strong guards at the gates. It is enclosed with walls and gates, but more for state than defense. The streets are large, running straight east and south, with channels and

rivers running through, which lose their waters into the Sea of Arima, as they call it, near a place of that name. The houses are but sorry and low, and, in the chief streets, fitted up for manufacturers and shopkeepers. The shops are hung, for ornament's sake, with black cloth. The inhabitants are very shortsized, but well-shaped, particularly the women, who are handsomer and better shaped, than I think in any other Asiatic country, but so much painted, that one would be apt to take them for wax figures, rather than living creatures. Their behavior is otherwise genteel, and the lively color of their lips is proof of their healthy complexion.

Saga was still large, very populous, its streets wide, dissected by narrow canals, and its women pretty, though thankfully no longer painted like wax figures.

The castle still had its moats, too. Its one surviving structure is its main gate, the imposing Shachi no Mon, which has been designated an Important National Cultural Property. Inside the *honmaru*, or 'inner citadel,' stood the Prefectural Saga Castle Museum. It was a faithful recreation of the former *goten*, or 'castle palace,' the building where its lord resided in times of peace.

Meeting the visitors entering the *genkan*, or 'entrance hall,' were blue and white banners with a diagonal border. The crest emblazoned on the white field confirmed they were the colors of the Nabeshima, the clan who ruled the Saga domain for most of its existence. There was no display related to the Nagasaki Kaidō, let alone the Edo Sanpu. But the permanent exhibition did go out of its way to explain the close link between the Saga domain and the Dutch factory in Nagasaki.

Chief propagator of those relations was the domain's tenth and penultimate lord, Nabeshima Naomasa (1815–71). Naomasa was a shrewd and cunning operator. Known as 'Mr. Facing-Both-Ways,' he spoke, according to the English diplomat Ernest Satow, 'in a fitful, abrupt manner accompanied by a tick whereby he constantly winked with both eyes.' It had been family circumstances that made Naomasa the man he was. Succeeding his profligate father at the age of

The rebuilt goten *on the grounds of Saga Castle*

seventeen, he became the lord of a domain on the verge of bankruptcy. Worse still, all his attempts at reform were thwarted by his retired father, who continued to hold sway over the domain's officials from behind the scenes. Things got so bad that when Naomasa visited Edo to see his cousin the *shōgun*, he was besieged by creditors.

Ironically, it was the destruction of his *goten* within the castle's second bailey that became the catalyst of his domain's recovery.

Moving his headquarters to the inner bailey, and furnished with a solid reason to economize, Naomasa did something unheard of. Like a veritable modern CEO, he began to lay off people, reducing the number of his samurai to a fifth of what it had been under his father.

But Naomasa wasn't done yet. He next set out to modernize his domain's academy. Founded in 1781 by his grandfather, the Kōdōkan was geared to the education of the domain's future officials. Yet its curriculum was built around the Chinese classics, Confucianist teachings, and traditional martial arts. In short, the academy was no longer equipped to deal with the domain's 19th-century challenges. And so Naomasa set out to turn the Kōdōkan into a modern academy that would teach his subjects to cope with a modern age. And it was here that he used his close contacts with the Dutch at Nagasaki.

It so happened that at the same time Naomasa set out to reform his Kōdōkan, the Nagasaki Naval Training Center opened its doors. It stood immediately behind Dejima Island and, though run by *bakufu* officials, it had Dutch teachers. Men like Pels Rijcken, Willem Hyussen van Kattendijke, and Johan Pompe van Meerdervoort instructed Japanese students in the Western sciences of shipbuilding, physics, chemistry, and medicine.

Saga's role in this initial spread of the latest Western sciences was disproportionally large. Out of the more than a hundred Japanese students at the Nagasaki Naval Training Center, forty-seven were from the Saga domain alone (as opposed to just sixteen from Satsuma and fifteen from Chōshū). To lord Naomasa it was the only way to deal with his domain's immediate challenges. Western medicine was needed to help his subjects suffering from smallpox. Western engineering was needed to build steamships and mass-produce cannon.

The urge of Naomasa and his fellow lords to catch up with the West came as a direct result of the arrival, in 1853, of Commodore Mathew Calbraith Perry's Black Ships in Edo Bay. Perry had come to reinforce America's demand that Japan open its ports to foreign trade. This act of Western gunboat diplomacy sent shockwaves through the realm. But in Kyushu, they were less surprised. Japan as a whole might have been cut off from the West for well over two

The Nagasaki Naval Training Center

centuries, but Kyushu's lords had dealt enough with the Europeans to know what they were capable of. So did Lord Naomasa.

Half a century earlier, his father had been in charge of Nagasaki's defense when, on 4 October 1808, an armed vessel flying a Dutch flag entered Nagasaki Bay. It proceeded to take hostage a number of Dutchmen who rowed out to meet the vessel. The vessel turned out to be British. It was HMS *Phaeton*, under the command of

41

Captain Fleetwood Pellew. He had entered Nagasaki Bay in the hope of ambushing some Dutch merchantmen. For the Brits, they were fair game. The Dutch Republic, after all, had been annexed by Napoleonic France, with which Britain was then at war. Yet it so happened that no Dutch vessels were expected to call at Nagasaki that year. And so, after Pellew had browbeaten the Nagasaki governor into provisioning his vessel in return for his Dutch hostages, HMS *Phaeton* departed again without a shot having been fired.

Damage had been done nevertheless. Unable to live with the shame of having given in to foreign threats, Nagasaki's governor Matsudaira Yasuhide committed ritual suicide. Naomasa's father survived, even though his profligacy had induced his elders to cut back on Nagasaki's defenses. Instead of the regular one thousand, Nagasaki had been defended by no more than a hundred samurai when HMS *Phaeton* entered its bay. Following a *bakufu* investigation, the Saga elders were also forced to commit ritual suicide. Naomasa's father was merely placed under house arrest for a hundred days. Yet the shadow of that shameful episode loomed large over Naomasa's youth.

Now, as Britain and other foreign nations were allowed to settle in Japanese ports, Naomasa and the other Kyushu lords knew what exactly that new 'foreign trade' might entail. Situated closest to the mainland, they had been the first to learn of the havoc the British were wreaking with their pernicious opium trade. They knew how the British kept pushing the drug upon the Chinese to further their cynical interests. And they knew how they had simply bombarded the port of Tingha when local authorities banned and seized their precious commodity. The Kyushu lords were determined that their domains, their people, Japan at large, would not share China's fate.

A team of Saga *rangakusha*, 'scholars of Dutch learning,' feverishly set to work translating a Dutch treatise on casting cannon, and work was begun on building the complex but required reverberatory furnace. Failure followed upon failure. But finally, in 1866, the first Saga-produced Armstrong cannon rolled off the production line.

By that time, events on the other side of Kyushu had taught Naomasa just how valuable such weapons might prove in the defense

Saga's reverbatory furnace

of his domain. Three years earlier, Satsuma, the most powerful domain on the island, had got its own taste of foreign gunboat diplomacy. Between 15 and 17 August 1863, a squadron of six British warships sailed up Kagoshima Bay and subjected Kagoshima to two bombardments after its lord had refused to pay compensation for the death of a British subject along the Tōkaidō (more about him later). It was only because Satsuma returned heavy fire from three gun

43

batteries in front of the town and three forts on the opposite shore that Rear-Admiral Augustus Kuyper decided to call it a day. That decision may well have been hastened by the damage wrought by Satsuma's cannon. Thirteen British sailors were killed in action and sixty-nine wounded. Among those killed were the captain and a senior officer of the flagship HMS *Eurialus*, whose heads were taken away by a Japanese cannonball just as they were briefing the admiral

The bombardment of Kagoshima

on the damage sustained to his ships. In the words of Ernest Satow, who was on board one of the ships, the British 'came away bitterly disappointed.'

It was not surprising, then, that Naomasa seized every single opportunity to learn from the West in order to counter the West. Already prior to the arrival of Commodore Perry, when the Dutch East India frigate *Palembang* entered Nagasaki Bay (with a letter from the Dutch king urging the *bakufu* to open its ports to foreign trade so Japan might not 'be destroyed by war'), he traveled down to Nagasaki and was invited aboard to take a tour of its decks. Impressed with what he saw, and with his father's traumatic experience in mind, Naomasa resolved to build his own steamship. That vision was realized in 1858, when he founded the Mietsu Naval Dock along the nearby Hayatsue River. There, his Dutch-trained engineers set about building Japan's

Saga's Ryōfū-maru

first steamship. In 1865, the sixty-feet Ryōfū-*maru* was launched by Naomasa in person.

Naomasa's relentless drive to push his domain and its people forward to meet the profound challenges of a modern, industrial age in which powerful countries grabbed by force what was not given freely went a long way to explain the epitaph he has earned among Saga's citizens: The Extraordinary Wise Ruler.

Kurume

The reception of the Mission in Kurume, according to Kaempfer, was decidedly more low-key than that in Saga. There, the crossroads along which it passed had been cordoned off by straw ropes to keep back hundreds of onlookers:

> We then came to Kurume, a large town of about two thousand houses. Entering the town we found the guard under arms, lining both sides of the street to some distance from the guard house. As soon as we came up to them, two of the soldiers put themselves at the head of our retinue, and two others behind to attend us in our passage through the town. The streets were washed before us, and there was not the least crowd to be seen, all the people keeping in the backside of their houses, where they saw us go by, kneeling, and in such a profound silence, that not the least noise was to be heard.
>
> We went by the place where public orders and proclamations are put up, not far from the ditch of the castle, where we saw a new proclamation put up lately, and twenty *shu* of silver nailed to the post, to be given as a reward to anybody that would discover the accomplices of a murder lately committed upon a dog. Many a poor man hath been severely punished in this country, under the present *shōgun*'s reign, purely for the sake of dogs.

A fondness for man's best friend seems to have run deep in the Arima, the clan whose members reigned over the Kurume domain for more than two centuries. Its eighth lord, Arima Yoritaka, collected special dog breeds, which he had delivered from Holland and brought along on his visits to Edo. Yet when I visited the Arima Museum on the grounds of Kurume Castle, I soon learned there was more to the Arima chieftains than Kaempfer might suggest.

Ishibashi-*san* was at least in his seventies, but since he had just started working as a museum guide, he considered himself a 'rookie.' I was the only visitor that afternoon, and though the exhibition area consisted of just a single large room, we spent the next hour chatting about the history of the Arima clan and their domain as we shuffled past the exhibits.

It quickly became clear that the Arima clan had been suffering the same economic hardship as the Nabeshima, though in their case through no fault of their own. Its first lord Arima Toyouji had been promoted to the domain in 1620 by *Shōgun* Tokugawa Ieyasu in reward for his contribution to the successful siege of Osaka Castle. He was even allowed to marry Ieyasu's daughter Renhime. The attending dowry was commensurate: it practically bankrupted his new domain from day one. For ten generations the Arima lords struggled to keep their domain financially afloat until, in 1844, Arima Yoritō came into office. Just twenty-two years old, young Yoritō carried through a raft of economic reforms and managed to make his domain solvent again. Like his neighbor Naomasa, he was an ardent student of Western learning and attracted important *rangakusha* to Kurume to help it modernize.

The Kurume domain also produced its own scholars. One such man was Tanaka Hisashige (1799–1881), the son of a tortoiseshell craftsman, he showed great promise at an early age. Imbued with a natural gift for engineering, Hisashige spent much of his youth making *karakuri*, or 'mechanical dolls.' In 1850 he moved to Kyoto to study Western engineering. The first fruit of that study was a myriad year clock that kept track of the Japanese hour, the Western hour, the day of the week, the month, and the moon phase—all by just winding it once a year. His clock can still be viewed at the National Museum of Nature and Science in Tokyo's Ueno Park.

Word of Hisashige's talents soon reached the ear of Saga's lord Nabeshima Naomasa, who hired him to help in the construction of

Hisashige demonstrates his miniature steam engine

a steam engine for his ship. The engineer acquitted himself well. After more diligent study at the new Dutch Naval Training Center in Nagasaki, he was able to demonstrate to his lord a working miniature steam engine on tracks within the grounds of Saga Castle.

Hisashige also assisted in the construction of Saga's reverberatory furnace. But in 1864, he returned to his native domain to help further his lord's policy to catch up with the West. By then, Yoritō was long dead. Just two years after embarking on his ambitious plan, the young lord died of uremia. He was just twenty-five. Of all Arima lords, Yoritō's rule was the shortest yet had the greatest impact.

Though modest in his choice of words, Ishibashi-*san* clearly took pride in the feats of his local heroes. And so he should. It was the exceptionally forward-looking leaders of Japan's western domains— led by Satsuma and Chōshū—who helped save Japan from a similar fate as China and led the way to Japan's rapid modernization.

The rest of the road from Kurume to the Hiyamizu Pass was flat and uneventful. It had been the same for the Mission. Occasionally, they would pass a town's execution grounds, which were invariably situated along the main traffic arteries to discourage potential criminals from carrying through their lawless designs:

> Between the second and third village, we saw a man lying on the cross, who was executed for having in a violent passion strangled a young boy to death, with his handkerchief, only because he had reprimanded him for stealing some wood. The crosses in this country are made, as Justus Lipsius [Joost Lips] relates in his Letters. A long cross-beam is placed at the upper end, on which are extended the arms, and another at the lower end for the feet of the malefactors. About the middle stands out another small piece of wood for them to sit on. They are not nailed, but tied to the cross with ropes.

Hiyamizu Pass

The next hurdle along the Nagasaki Kaidō toward Kokura was the

Hiyamizu-*tōge*, the old pass across the Sangun-*sanchi*, a mountain range that stretches inland just north of Fukuoka. It derives its name from the three districts (*sangun*) on which it borders—Kasuya, Chikushi, and Kaho.

Slowly I made my way toward the pass, the second ascent after the one toward Ureshino. As I trudged uphill, my admiration for the Japanese porters carrying the *kago*, or 'palanquins,' in which the Westerners were riding grew with each step. Dressed in little more than a loincloth, they actually jogged along while they carried their heavy burden on bare shoulders. Being taller and often more corpulent as a result of their sedentary life on Dejima Island, the Mission's members were considerably heavier than your average Japanese dignitary, and the thought of having to carry a load of some forty kilos up the slope on a single shoulder made my ten-kilo, ergonomically harnessed rucksack weigh like a feather.

Being a man of his time, Kaempfer seems to have had little eye for his porters. He seemed more concerned with the inconvenience this mode of travel imposed on himself, rather than those who had to carry him:

> After dinner we set out again in *kago*, because of the neighboring hills and mountains, we were now to travel over, and which are not easily to be passed on horseback. It is a very incommodious way of traveling in these *kago*, they being like small square baskets, open on all sides and only covered with a small roof, to which is fastened the pole.

Fischer voiced similar sentiments but had more eye for the fate of the porters:

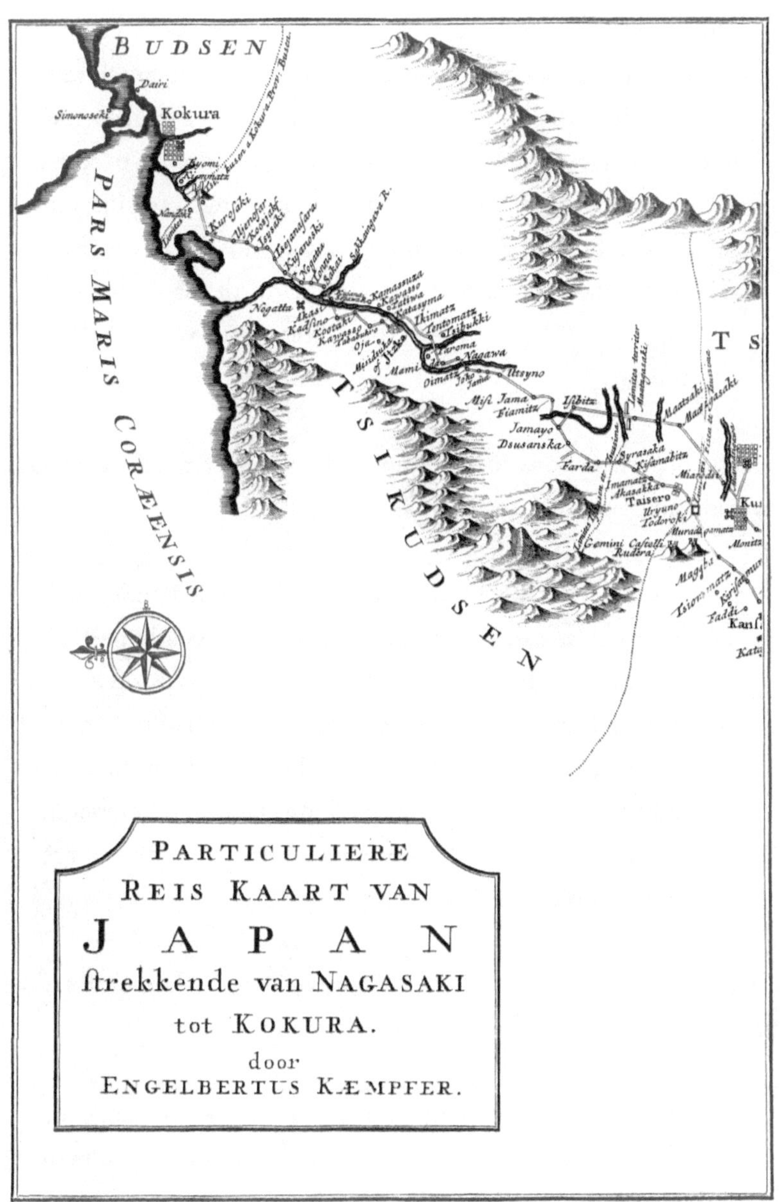

The route from Kurume to Kokura

On the 11th, we had a difficult passage across the Hiyamizu Mountains [sic.] as the roads had been exposed to much rain and were hard to pass for the porters. As usual, we stayed a few hours at a place by the same name to treat our friends to some *sake*, which is done to enable the train of porters carrying our gifts and other heavy luggage to get ahead. Otherwise, we would overtake them and, arriving all at the same time to exchange porters and horses, the whole thing would end in confusion.

Siebold, perhaps conscious of his weight, was also more considerate. Already en route to Ureshino, he noted that:

It feels uncomfortable for us travelers to be carried under such conditions by men who are exhausted by the weight and the heat. And it is perhaps a good thing that they do not feel the humiliating harshness of their condition, for when they have quenched their burning thirst with the water from buckets placed in front of the farmhouses along the road, they begin among each other jocular conversations in which we are usually the topic.

By the time they reached the Hiyamizu Pass, his discomfort had turned to a mixture of pity and admiration:

The deeper we entered the mountains, the less passable the roads became because of the relentless rain. I pitied the men and animals, even though I admired the agility and confidence with which they climb narrow, steep, and slippery slopes.

Without their footwear it would have been impossible for them to carry along loads on such roads. The straw sandals, therefore, are a requirement in this country that cannot be replaced by leather shoes and horseshoes.

Unlike in the West, in Japan, horses were made to wear the same kind of straw sandals as humans. Called *umagutsu*, they had braided

The entrance to the Hiyamizu Pass

strands by which they were tied around the animal's ankles. As can be imagined, what with the weight of a horse and the conditions of the roads, such footwear did not last long, and most of the stops while crossing a pass were dictated by the need to change *umagutsu*.

Bits of the old path leading up toward the pass were still intact, though most of it had meanwhile been asphalted. I preferred the old paving but had to admit that it would have eased the jobs of the

53

Japanese porters and horses, whose only footwear were straw sandals.

Though lightly packed and walking in perfect weather, I was quite exhausted when I reached the top of the pass myself. It was marked by the old boundary posts demarcating the border between the Fukuoka domain of Kuroda Nagamasa (1568–1623), and the small Akitsuki domain of his third son Kuroda Nagaoki (1610–65). Joining the top of the pass on the left-hand side was a long flight

Toward the crest of the Hiyamizu Pass

of stairs. It passed under an arch of multiple red *torii* toward the Onechi-*jinja*, the shrine that sits at the crest of the eponymous mountain.

When I began to descend the path toward Uchino, I found the first seven hundred yards of the old high road completely intact. Just like old sections of the Nakasendō I had walked six years before, it was paved with large granite boulders, not unlike those used in castle
54

walls. It is said that the pass was paved on the orders of Kuroda Nagamasa. If this is true, his men did a very good job. The flat surfaces of the large boulders were all made to lie level and carefully interlocked to create a perfectly paved road. At one section, an old bridge crafted from a long granite slab across a mountain brook was also intact. It was from its 'cool waters' that the pass derived its name, for that is what the word *hiyamizu* means. The place was guarded

The stone bridge and the 'headles' jizō

(according to a nearby notice board) by a *kubi nashi jizō*, a 'headless *jizō*.' Yet the statue definitely still had its head on. Perhaps it had been glued back on at some stage.

It seems the northern slopes of the Sangun Mountains were teeming with wildfowl in Fischer's day. Having safely made it downhill, he was treated to pheasant and wild duck eggs. Four years later, while Siebold and the rest of the Mission descended the same mountain path:

We were surprised by a pheasant that flew up with the sound of a black grouse. We could not make out whether it was a *yamadori* or a *kiji*. Both, by the way, are said to be very common among these mountains.

The encounter put the otherwise scientifically inclined German in a poetic frame of mind, recalling lines from a poem by Ōtomo no Yakamochi (718–785). whose poems found their way into the *Manyōshū*, the famed anthology of *waka* poetry compiled during the Nara period. Perhaps they did so because he compiled it. In 767, Yakamochi was appointed to the Dazaifu, so he might well have come across the same pheasants while traversing the Hiyamizu Pass:

Haru no no asaru
kigishi no tsumagoi ni,
ono ga atari wo
hito ni shiretsutsu

In a spring meadow
The green pheasant,
rummaging for feed,
Cries for his mate,
It cries, 'Here am I'
To a nearby hunter.

Sadly, no pheasant, copper or green, cried 'here am I,' as I made my long descent into Uchino. Perhaps they had wised up and learned to lay low whenever a human crossed their way, though I did hear the call of a Japanese bush warbler: '*uuuuuuuuguisu!*'

Uchino

I also ran into a fellow traveler. Walking into Uchino a man in proper hiking gear with a walking stick greeted me enthusiastically. Imaeda-*san* was a young-looking seventy-year-old pensioner from Nagoya with a sunny disposition. His story was less sunny. Ten years earlier, he had been diagnosed with stomach cancer. He had come through.

The Uchinomatsu Shrine

Partly, he said, because he had taken up walking on his doctor's advice. Since then, he had walked the Tōkaidō twice, the Shikoku Henrō once, and now he was walking the Nagasaki Kaidō. He hadn't walked them in one fell swoop but in stages, using his free weekends to do successive sections.

Uchino was a pleasant town that took pride in its post-town history. Though only a few old buildings remained, many houses had signposts in front of them boasting their historic credentials. One, called the Nagasaki-*ya*, claimed to have been visited by none other than Siebold, though it did concede the present structure was built during the Meiji period.

I rested on the grounds of the Uchinooimatsu Shrine and ate the sandwiches I had packed that morning. I was happy I had met Imaeda-*san*. I was happy to be alive.

Kokura

Little of today's Kokura—now part of the huge city of Kita Kyushu—would remind Siebold or Fischer, let alone Kaempfer, of the town through which they passed long ago. The only exception perhaps is the remains of Kokura Castle. But even this they might not recognize. For one, because its original keep looked quite different from today's ferro-cement reconstruction, which is based on a different design. More likely they would not recognize it because they never got to see it from close up. The surrounding castle grounds occupied an area of three million square yards and were surrounded by high walls. The Mission's members stayed in lodgings safely outside these walls, in the castle town east of the stronghold, on the opposite bank of the Murasaki River's wide mouth.

If they thought they might get a glimpse inside Kokura's castle walls during a pleasant visit and be treated to a cup of tea with its lord they would have been mistaken. The best they could hope for was a rendezvous with one of his lordship's 'envoys.' This is what happened to *Opperhoofd* Johan Willem de Sturler, with whom Siebold was traveling, but even this turned out to be a disappointment:

Immediately upon our arrival, his lordship's envoy announced himself, and since the *opperhoofd* was not yet ready to receive him, Mr. Bürger and I had the honor of receiving our guest. We were, however, rather disappointed to find that our honored guest turned out to be little more than the guard of the castle's gate and, to boot, a truly simple-minded fellow, who had little more of importance to say than that his lordship was not at home but at the *shōgun*'s court in Edo.

And so the Mission's members had to while away their time at the Ōsaka-*ya*, the local *honjin* and the usual place where the Dutch were put up before they would be ferried over to Shimonoseki. That stay grew all the more tedious when bad weather prevented them from crossing the strait. This happened to Dirk de Graeff van Polsbroek, who passed through Kokura on 18 March 1859 with Factor Janus Henricus Donker Curtius. He had been thrilled at the sight of open water, but was forced to spend one day and night at the inn because of a raging storm:

> That day's stay at Kokura was surprisingly boring. Walking around in our hotel or *honjin*, my attention was drawn to carvings in the beams, the cornices of doors, and even in the wooden furniture, carved by Dutch *opperhoofd*s of the factory of Dutch trade at Dejima, who made the journey many years before us and who had probably also been bored at Kokura, just like us. All had been preserved with the greatest piety.

None of the carvings so piously preserved have survived. Allied bombing and the general march of time have ensured that nothing is left of Kokura's former castle town, let alone the inn at which the Mission's members stayed and left their graffiti. I felt justified, therefore, to take up my own lodging, not in Kokura but in Shimonoseki, on the other side of the eponymous strait. It was a place, after all, the Mission had visited and a place that had more to offer in historic terms.

Before I took the ferry to Shimonoseki, I wanted to visit the Mojikō

Mojikō Station, the heart of the Mojikō District

Retro District. Situated a few miles farther east along the strait from Kokura, the Port of Moji was developed in 1889 by the Meiji statesman Suematsu Kenchō (1855–1920) to ship coal from central Fukuoka Province to the rest of the country. To realize his project, Kenchō approached the industrialist Shibusawa Eiichi (1840–1931), who in turn mobilized the economic clout of the Mitsui Company, which built its own clubhouse in the port during the Taishō period (1912–26).

60

The old Moji Mitsui Club is still there. As are a number of other Meiji- and Taishō-era buildings. The clubhouse stands opposite Mojikō Station, which itself is a Taishō period structure said to have been inspired by Rome's former Termini Station. Next to the old clubhouse stand the old Mojikō Post Office and the old Mitsui O.S.K. Lines Ltd. Building. Behind them lies the Mojikō Marina. Along it stand the former Mojikō Customs Office and the International Friendship Memorial Library. The latter is an almost exact copy of the offices the Imperial Russian Railway built in the Chinese port of Dalian when it was under their control during the early 20th century (it now houses the Dalian Art Gallery).

Though established only in 1995 as a tourist attraction with modern amenities and a high-tech drawbridge, Mojikō Retro District's spacious layout gives ample scope to the old buildings. Combined with the wholesome seaside air, it breathes a pleasant and genuine historic atmosphere that would make Walt Disney jealous.

Strait of Shimonoseki

Siebold describes the crossing of the Strait of Shimonoseki in great detail: the depths at different sections, its geographical features, and many other things of note. One was a monument to a certain Akashi Yojibei, a skipper who is said to have endangered the life of Toyotomi Hideyoshi by grounding his vessel whilst ferrying the despot across the strait. To atone for his sins, Yojibei disemboweled himself. Not long afterward, the new lord of Kokura Castle, Hosokawa Tadaoki (1563–1645), erected a stone monument to the skipper on the nearby shore. It now sits in the southwest corner of Mekari Park.

Otherwise, Siebold only mentions the nearby island of Funa-*jima*, on the opposite shore. He does so only in passing—quite literally so:

> As soon as one has passed Funa-*jima*, one's field of view widens, and the coast of Buzen joins with that of Nagato and Hikoshima to present a delightful panorama.

The Strait of Shimonoseki

Most Japanese today are more familiar with Funa-*jima* than Yojibei's rock, let alone his sad story. Funa-*jima*, after all, is the island where the famed swordsman Miyamoto Musashi defeated his great rival Sasaki Kojirō. Kojirō was a practitioner of the Ganryū school of swordsmanship, hence its modern name of Ganryū Island.

A native of Harima Province (Hyōgo Prefecture), Musashi often crossed the strait, as his father lived in the port of Nakatsu, some thirty miles east along the coast from Kokura. It was during one of these crossings that, staying with an old friend, he learned that among the many fencing instructors of Hosokawa Tadaoki was a swordsman whose skills were said to be unsurpassed. This clashed with his own world view, in which his own skills were unsurpassed. Thus it was that, on 13 May 1612, at the hour of the Dragon (7:00), the two men met in duel on Funa-*jima*. Musashi had himself ferried over to the

A bronze statue portrays the 'historic' encounter

island from Shimonoseki. He was late. The wily swordsman dallied on purpose: making his opponents wait and grow agitated was one of his strategies. Another was to craft one of the ferryman's oars into a weapon with which he crushed Kojirō's skull in a single blow.

A far more important event in Japan's long martial history took place just a sea mile farther up the straight, at an inlet called Dan no Ura. The Sea Battle of Dan no Ura was the culminating battle of the

Genpei War (1180–85), the epic struggle for supremacy between the Heike and the Minamoto clans.

Among the many Heike vessels was that of the young Emperor Antoku. Only seven years old, the boy was accompanied by a retinue of court ladies. Eager to learn how the sea battle was going, they anxiously awaited the arrival of the vessel of the Middle Counselor Tomomori, who was just then making his way toward the imperial vessel. When he came within earshot, they all cried out, 'How is the battle faring Lord Tomomori? How are we doing?'

Aware the Minamoto were about to win, the counselor burst out laughing and sarcastically replied, 'You will soon be getting acquainted with some curious eastern warriors.'

At this, the court ladies began to shriek in panic and retorted, 'Why are you making jokes at a time like this?'

One of the court ladies was Taira no Tokiko. She was the wife of Taira no Kiyomori and the young emperor's grandmother. Turning to her grandson she said, 'Due to bad karma, your luck has run out. Now turn to the east and say farewell to the Great Shrine of Ise. Then face west and offer up a prayer to the Buddha.'

The *Heike monogatari*, from which the above scene was taken, goes on to describe the boy's last moments:

He wore a cape the color of the mountain-dwelling turtledove and had his hair tied up in braids on each side of his head. He choked on his tears as he joined his dainty hands together in prayer, turned toward the east, and prostrated himself to say farewell to the Great Shrine of Ise. Next, he turned to the west and offered up a prayer to the Buddha. Then, clutching the young emperor in her arms, Tokiko cried out, 'There is a city below the waves for us!' at which she cast herself and the boy into the boundless depths.

Shimonoseki

Though Shimonoseki was just a small town in Kaempfer's time, it already was an important port:

> The Town of Shimonoseki itself consists of four to five hundred houses, built chiefly on both sides of one long street, which runs quite through, there being but a few smaller streets, which turn off sideways, and all terminate into this great one. The city is full of shops, wherein are sold victuals and provision for ships, which daily put in there in great numbers. Upon our arrival, there were no less than two hundred, great and small, lay there at anchor, it being the common harbor for ships bound from the western provinces to the eastern, or coming from these.

In stark contrast with the cold reception at Kokura, the Mission's reception at Shimonoseki, according to Siebold, was very warm:

> During its stay at Shimonoseki, the Mission is housed in the residence of one of the port's two mares, who both take turns in sharing the honor. This time around, we stayed with Sakō-*sama*, whose spacious hotel is located in the Nabe Township, near the quay where we disembarked. We received a very warm reception from the landlord and his family and were

put up in very reasonable accommodations. Shortly after our arrival, the other mare presented himself—an enthusiastic supporter of the Dutch, who announced himself as such by means of his calling card, for on it was written: Van den Berg.

Four years earlier, Fischer had also met with the Holandophile:

Though he did not speak a word of Dutch, he took great delight in learning Dutch manners and acquiring all kinds of curiosities. These he kept in a hidden room, and among them were very old things that had been collected over many years and arranged in a most remarkable fashion. He had sufficient of these artifacts at hand on the first afternoon to supply us with what we needed. And at night, when he was really in the mood, he dressed up in Dutch costume, which was no less curious than his Dutch collection!

I decided to take a rest and booked myself three nights in a row at the pleasant Uzu House, right along the strait's northern shore. I arrived late in the afternoon and was starving but I wasn't willing to pay the tourist prices they were asking at the restaurants along Shimonoseki's luxurious Kamon Wharf Promenade. And so I strolled into the jaded downtown area. I found a nice old place where they served a good *yakisoba* for just ¥600, less than $5.

Behind the counter sat an old man who could have played the sage in a classic Kung Fu movie. His voice needn't be dubbed either. He spoke the most mellifluous English, though he said it was getting rusty. I asked him if he had lived abroad, but no, it was just what he had learned in high school. He must have been a very bright student.

66

Oji-*san* had worked in the family restaurant for seventy years and had started out at sixteen. He had seen Shimonoseki grow and change, much of it while fishing on the banks of the Koseto, or 'Small Strait,' the narrow strait that runs north and parallel to its bigger sister. The best time to fish, he said, is at night, when the fish draw closer to the shore. Above the table at which I was enjoying my *yakisoba* and draft beer, hung what looked like an Indian ink drawing

*Oji-*san *in front of his* gyōtaku

of a huge fish. I remarked on it and asked Oji-*san* if he had drawn it himself—it was stunningly accurate.

'That's a *gyōtaku*,' he said smiling benevolently at my ignorance. It's a fish print. 'You rub the fish you catch with Indian ink and then press on a sheet of dampened *washi* paper. I only used to do it when I had a really great catch. That one was a *madai*, a red sea bream. It was eighty-two centimeters, one of the biggest I ever caught.'

67

'I suppose you had a real feast meal,' I replied.

Again he smiled gently. 'The big ones aren't very tasty, it's the small ones you want to eat.'

I asked Oji-*san* to stand next to the print so I could take his photograph. He did so proudly. I wondered how many more years he would greet his customers with his pleasant voice and how long, amid Shimonoseki's rapid modernization, his restaurant would survive.

The Japanese ship of war JS Akizuki *docked near Shimonoseki's ferris wheel*

I wasn't in Shimonoseki just to eat *yakisoba*. For some reason, the port town was one of the few stops at which the Mission's members could stroll around freely and at length, especially if they had to wait for favorable weather to cross the Inland Sea.

One fixed item on the agenda was the Amida Temple. Kaempfer, Blomhoff, Siebold, and Fissher all visited the 'famed temple' during their stay at Shimonoseki. All mistakenly claim the temple was built in memory of 'Prince' Antoku. In truth, the temple had already guarded the straight for more than two centuries by the time Antoku drowned. It was founded in 859 by the Heian monk Gyōkyō, and was a so-called *chinjūsha*, a Shintō shrine built on Buddhist temple grounds and dedicated to a tutelary local deity. In the case of the Amida Temple, it was dedicated to Hachiman, the God of War. It was probably for that reason that its grounds were

The Akama Shrine, alias Amida Temple

allegedly chosen to bury Antoku's remains. Yet it is not at all certain that the infant's remains rest at the temple. Indeed, many other places in Japan claim the same honor. Some sources even suggest that he survived the battle and that, spirited away by remnants of the Heike clan, he went into hiding—in Settsu according to some, in Inaba, according to others, on the island of Kyushu by others yet. Who can say?

It was during the 1870s that the Meiji government seized the temple's association with the imperial family to change it into a Shintō shrine. The true motive behind the move was their policy of *shinbutsu bunri*, a dormant Edo period movement that advocated the 'separation of Shintō and Buddhism.' One reason why the Meiji leaders chose to adopt the policy was to curtail the wealth and power of the Buddhist sects. The other goal was to strengthen the Shintō religion. Being an indigenous religion that fostered an emperor cult, Shintō proved a perfect vehicle to boost the desired love of country. Thousands of temples were forcibly closed, their grounds confiscated, their monks forced to return to secular life.

Thus it was that the Amida Temple became the Akama Shrine, 'Akama,' or 'Red Gate,' being an old name (Akamagaseki) for the Strait of Shimonoseki. As such, the Akama Shrine is not only a monument to the port's long history but also a reminder of one of the more pernicious policies of the early Meiji government, a policy that set the country on its disastrous road toward nationalism, militarism, and eventually war.

Inland Sea

The Inland Sea, or Seto Naikai as it is called in Japan, has been used as a traffic artery as long as the Japanese Isles have been populated by humans.

Kitamae-bune *on the Inland Sea*

Even when the first network of high roads was established during the Nara period ships continued to sail its waters to carry heavy or bulky goods from one port to the other. During the Warring States period (1467–1615), when seafaring clans raided merchantmen or extorted taxes before they let them pass, traffic over water became dangerous. But when, in 1588, Toyotomi Hideyoshi issued an edict banning all piracy in Japanese waters, the Inland Sea grew into the busiest maritime traffic lane in the realm.

71

The Inland Sea, from Morotsu to Mitarai

*Though ships crossed the Inland Sea in a wide web that connected the
many ports along its coasts, wind conditions and the development of large
traffic hubs naturally led to the vessels following fixed routes. At first,
most of the seaborne trade remained confined to the Inland Sea. But during
the Edo Period, the naval traffic arteries stretched to reach ports that lay
on Japan's coasts facing the Pacific and the Sea of Japan. The most famous
among these traffic arteries ran from Osaka to Shimonoseki and from there
all the way to the northern port of Ishikari in far-away Ezo, today's
Hokkaidō.*

The ships that sailed this busy sea route were called kitamae-bune *or
'north-bound ships.' Most of them were of a type called* bezai-sen, *round-
hulled and carvel-planked vessels with junk-type rigging. Hundreds upon
hundreds of these vessels used to populate the Japanese waters, carrying
northward rice, rapeseed, sugar, salt,* sake, *paper, candle wax, straw, and
fabric; and bringing back dried herring, salmon, sardines, and kelp.*

Mitarai

One of the Mission's first ports of call upon entering the Inland Sea
was Mitarai. Situated on the east tip of Ōsakishimo Island and
protected from the east winds by Okamura Island, the port had been
a safe haven as long as man-made vessels crossed the Inland Sea. One
dignitary to visit the port was the legendary Empress Jungū, who
was on her way to invade the Korean Peninsula. It is said that while
ashore, she washed her hands at a local well. This lent the place its
name, for *mitarai* means 'the honorable washing of hands.'

Despite being a small port on a small island, Mitarai seems to have
been a place of considerable culture. Fischer mentions how:

Around noon the wind veered to the west and we were forced to drop our anchor in front of Mitarai. There we spent the night after we had attended a Japanese *sake* party, on which occasion we listened to a number of *shamisen* players from Hiroshima. Yet I must confess that we did not take any delight in this music nor in anything similar we had heard hitherto. We did, however, admire the punctual order and the honor that was shown to us, since all who were out on the streets bowed until we had passed. As we did so, two persons with broomsticks went ahead of the train shouting, '*Shita ni! Shita ni!*' to notify them of our approach and to remove the tiniest stones or debris from the road.

Nowadays, Ōsakishimo and Okamura, through a string of other islands, are connected to the Honshū mainland (if one can call it that) by some seven bridges. But since the Dutch had crossed the Inland Sea by boat, and since it was much more fun to experience it from the water, I took a ferry.

The high-speed ferry service between the port of Takehara and Mitarai was run by men who knew what they were doing. As soon as the boat was out in the open sea, it picked up a formidable speed, only to slow down and blow its horn when it approached one of the five stops along the way. If someone was waiting on one of the floating piers, the captain dexterously maneuvered the vessel alongside. Then his mate would jump ashore, tie the vessel up aft and, while the captain drove the rope taught by opening the throttle, lower the hydrolic gangplank just long enough for the new passenger to hop on board. It was a routine they must have practiced a million times.

Walking into Mitarai I was going back in time. The well where the empress washed her hands was still there, as was much of the village encountered by the Dutch Missions on their way to Edo. As at Uchino, most of the old houses had signposts boasting their pedigree: the type of architecture, the time of construction, and the families that lived in them at present. The houses generally dated back to the late 18th or early 19th century and were either built in

Mitarai, one of the Mission's first ports of call

the simple *kirizuma* (gable roof) or the more complex *irimoya* (hip and gable roof) tradition.

I was studying a large signboard with a map that stood on the south side of the village facing the island of Shikoku, when a little girl appeared. She began to ask me questions: Where was I from? What language did people speak there? What was I doing here? Her questions answered, she picked up a stick and began to point out various places of interest on the map: 'This is the well where people wash their hands.' 'This is the Ebisu Shrine.' 'And this is the house of Tom, the Englishman.' I hadn't read anything about an Englishman. Could it be that, despite the Dutch being the only ones allowed to stay on during Japan's long period of seclusion, an English sailor had managed to slip through the net? Like the famed pilot William Adams, who had become an advisor to *Shōgun* Tokugawa Ieyasu?

Much of the village has remained unchanged since the Edo period

I was intrigued as the map did not give any information on the subject. I asked the girl to lead me to Tom's house. It stood just a stone's throw away. She reached up and rang the doorbell. Presently a young woman appeared. She greeted the girl as if she knew her but looked somewhat puzzled at me. 'Is Tom-*san* in?' the girl asked, and I realized my mistake. Tom, who now also stepped outside, was alive and kicking; not some historic figure. Wearing a T-shirt, shorts, and flip-flops, he looked bemused as he sipped intermittently on a vaper he was holding between his thumb and index finger while he measured me up with sympathetic yet critical eyes. I apologized and explained my folly. But they didn't seem to mind at all and asked me what had brought me to Mitarai. When I told them, Tom mentioned that he, too, was working on a book. It dealt with Japan's aging problem and its rapidly emptying countryside.

As I left, they wished me a safe journey. I said I was looking forward to reading his book, which I was, since it dealt with an important topic.

Reading up about Tom later, I realized Mitarai did have an English resident of note; an award-winning documentary maker and an established author who has written a number of books for renowned publishing houses.

Speeding back to Takehara, the air suddenly cleared and in the distance among the islands, I could see all the way toward the narrowest part of the Inland Sea, toward the Kurushima Strait and its huge suspension bridge. It was the route the Dutch used to take from Mitarai before they headed back toward the Honshū mainland and the port of Tomonoura.

Abuto Kannon

Though not a port of call, an important milestone on the Mission's journey across the Inland Sea was the Abuto Kannon. The old temple sits at the tip of the Numakuma Hantō, the peninsula on which also lies Tomonoura. Already in Kaempfer's time, Tomonoura was a fixed port of call and the Abuto Kannon a beacon to look out for:

About a quarter of a German mile before you come to the village, stands a famous temple of the idol Abuto, which is said to be very eminent for miraculously curing many inveterate distempers, as also for procuring a favorable wind and good passage. For this reason, sailors and passengers always tie some farthings to a piece of wood, and throw it into the sea as an offering to this Abuto Kannon-*sama*, or Lord God Abuto, as they call him, in order to obtain from him a favorable wind. The priest of the temple says that these offerings never fail to drive on shore, and to come safe to his hands. However, for caution's sake, he comes out himself in still weather in a small boat, to ask this sort of tribute to his idol, of what ships and boats sail by.

I intended to take the first ferry from Onomichi to Tsuneishi, on the west side of the Numakuma Peninsula, but discovered I didn't have the small change to buy myself a ticket from the vending machine. The booth was still closed so I ran down the pier to ask the skipper what to do. He immediately jumped ashore and told me to follow him. Then he dived into his office to retrieve his wallet and gave me the change from my bill of ¥10.000. It was one of those small acts of kindness with which my journey through Japan would be filled.

Disembarking at Tsuneishi, I found its inhabitants to be a merry lot. As they passed me, walking and cycling into work at its shipyards, almost half of them greeted me with a cheerful '*Ohaiyō gozaimasu!*' wishing me a good morning I had not heard in other places. And none of them wore face masks, so Tsuneishi came out well above the national average.

78

After a stiff hour's walk, I reached the tip of the Numakuma Peninsula. There, the Abuto Kannon still watched over those who passed it on their way to their destination. To give it a hand in aiding navigation, a modern lighthouse higher up on the cliff now casts its searching beams over the Inland Sea at night.

The Abuto Kannon is said to have been erected more than a thousand years ago by Emperor Kazan (968–1008). It was built in

The Abuto Kannon

honor of Ekādaśamukha, the Eleven-faced Bodhisattva, so it would watch over his seafaring subjects. Its protection was lost during the Genpei War, when the adjacent temple was burned down and the statue cast into the waves below. But in 1338 a fisherman from nearby Tomonoura had a vision in his dream that he should retrieve the statue. He set out in his boat and cast his net out in the waters just off the cape. And lo and behold, in his net, he found the Abuto

Kannon. It was put back on its pedestal and has continued to protect the local sailors ever since. The temple, too, was resurrected. It was rebuilt by Mōri Terumoto (1553–1625), the most powerful warlord in western Honshū, who is said to have commanded a fleet of a thousand sails.

The Kannon not only protected sailors. Inside the dark recesses of the little shrine atop the structure, countless votive tablets, pieces of

Votive tablets inside the Aboto Kannon

wood not unlike those that had been cast into the sea by sailors, hung suspended from the rafts. Attached to them were not farthings but pairs of comely shaped female breasts, with short texts praying for a fruitful pregnancy and speedy delivery.

At the foot of the stairs, on the south side of the structure, I noticed a narrow path leading up the cliff face. Always in for an adventure, I began to trace it, hoping it might be a shortcut along the coast toward Tomonoura. As I progressed, the path began to rise and narrow until it was no more than a mountain goat's trail, less than a foot wide and high above the rocks and surf below. At one particularly precarious section, someone had suspended a nylon rope between a few branches that sprang from the cliff face. I was scared out of my wits, but realizing it was the price one had to pay to still find a bit of pristine beach on the Inland Sea, I pressed on.

My struggle paid off. At length, the trail descended again and I happened onto a stretch of beach with not a soul in sight. The only sign of civilization was a single fishing boat moored off the coast, bobbing up and down on a gentle swell.

I donned my clothes and plunged into the cool blue water. I swam away from the shore until I could no longer feel the sand and pebbles below my feet. Several times I dived down, fancying I might happen on some farthings that had come loose from their little rafts and drifted to the seabed. I was almost disappointed not to find any, the reason being explained by Siebold, who noted that:

> The countless offerings are retrieved by fishermen who are in
> the service of the monks of the Abuto Kannon.

Tomonoura

A *tonbi*, a 'black kite,' kept diving down at me as I skirted the new marina on the west side of Tomonoura. It was probably preying on the *onigiri* filled with grilled salmon flakes I was eating, so I broke a bit off and tossed it up into the air. It tried to catch it but the morsel fell to the ground where it was snatched up by a quayside cat. The scene caused great hilarity among an elderly couple sitting outside a nearby fishmonger. 'Did the *tonbi* attack you?' the old lady laughed.

'Yes,' I said, 'back home they are far less daring.'

'They're terrible,' she groaned. 'I can't cross the street with a morsel of fish without them attacking me. I'm terrified of them!'

After Mitarai, Tomonoura was the Mission's second large port of call on their route through the Inland Sea. Kaempfer describes how, having navigated the Kurushima Strait under Shikoku's shore, they steered north-northeast toward the Abuto Kannon, from where they followed the shore of the Numakuma Peninsula eastward to the port:

> On our starboard side, there was almost nothing but water, so far as we could see, being a large gulf, which runs in between Iko and Sanuki, the two northern provinces of the Island of Shikoku. It runs in so deep between the said two provinces, that we could not see to the end of it. On our larboard side, we saw several villages upon the great Island of Honshū. Not far from there, we came to the famous harbor and village of Tomonoura, which we had on our larboard side, at a very small distance. It lies upon the continent of Honshū, in the province of Bingo, from whence it is called Bingo no Tomo, for distinction's sake from a village of the same name. It lies on a rising ground at the foot of the mountain and consists of some hundred houses, which made a pretty good appearance, being built around the harbor, which is nearly semicircular.

It was the bay's shape that lent Tomonoura its name. In the eyes of the ancient Japanese, it resembled the comma-like shape of a *tomo*, an archer's left-wrist protector. Its history is said to go all the way back to the Yayoi period (10th to 3rd centuries BC), though at that time it was probably just a primitive settlement whose dwellers lived from what the sea provided. Tomonoura's history as a port goes back to the early Nara period, when the court noble and General of the Left Ōtomo no Tabito (665–731), father to the man who immortalized the pheasants along the Hiyamizu Pass, sang the port's praise. It seems

The ancient port of Tomonoura

that Tabito (which literally means 'traveler') called at the port several times. He did so on his way to and back from Kyushu, first in 720, when he was ordered to quash the rebellion of the indigenous Hayato tribe, and again in 728, when he was appointed head of the Dazaifu. On that occasion, he was accompanied by his wife, and it was her death whilst there, that threw him into a state of desperate longing when, on his return, his ship passed the sights they had enjoyed so much together on their way out. Especially Tomonoura seems to have left a deep impression on the couple, for two of his poems (both included in the *Manyōshū*) are dedicated to the port:

Wagimoko ga mishi
tomonoura no muro no ki wa,
tokoyo ni aredo
mishihitozo naki

My beloved wife
Saw that juniper at Tomonoura
Now that I return,
The tree remains,
Yet no more is she.

Tomonoura no iso no
muro no ki,
mimugoto ni
ahimishi imo wa
wasurae me yamo.

Whenever I see that juniper
On the rocks at Tomonoura,
I remember my wife
Who enjoyed it with me
How can I forget her?

In front of the lighthouse, at the head of a short pier that forms the indent in the port's comma-shaped harbor, stands the *Iroha-maru*

Exhibition Hall. Housed in a traditional gable-roofed building, its permanent exhibition is dedicated to the shipwreck of the *Iroha-maru*. On 26 May 1867, the cargo vessel sank off nearby Mu Island, whilst being towed toward the port after it had collided with the steamship *Meikō-maru* of the Kishū domain on the Ise Peninsula.

The seabed of the Inland Sea is littered with plenty of shipwrecks. What makes the *Iroha-maru* stand out was the presence on board of

Tomonoura's old lighthouse and the Iroha-maru Exhibition Hall

one of Japan's national heroes: Sakamoto Ryōma (1836–67). The scion of a lowly samurai family from the Tosa domain in Shikoku, Ryōma was one of the most flamboyant figures of the *bakumatsu* period (1853–67), the dying years of the Tokugawa *bakufu*. That period was ushered in by the arrival of Commodore Perry's black ships and ended with the overthrow of the *bakufu* in the Boshin War by a coalition of Satsuma and Chōsho forces. It had been Ryōma

Sakamoto Ryōma, his eyes confidently fixed on a future filled with promise

who, in 1864, had united the two domains—once fierce enemies—
in their effort to establish a Western-style government. It had been
Ryōma, too, whose shipping company Kaientai chartered the vessel.
And it was Ryōma who, on 22 May 1867, commanded the vessel
when it set sail from Nagasaki bound for Osaka.

The one big question that has loomed over the *Iroha-maru* ever
since it sank is the identity of its cargo. Many believe it was carrying
weapons to be used against the *bakufu* in the Boshin War. Whatever
it was, it certainly wasn't straw hats. During the subsequent
negotiations held at Tomonoura, Ryōma and his fellow Kaientai
members demanded (and received) reparations for the cargo to the
tune of 47,896 *ryō*. Though by then the *ryō* had devalued massively
as a result of the political instability, it still amounted to the rough
equivalent of $1 million in today's money.

In 1988, the mystery seemed to be on the verge of being solved
when divers from the Tomo o Aisuru Kai, the Association of Tomo
Lovers, discovered the wreck some seven sea miles out at sea. For
days, the whole nation was glued to the television screen as one item
after the other was retrieved from the ship's badly damaged and
decomposing hull. Yet apart from some brass door hinges and coat
pegs, nothing lethal was found. In the eyes of the conspirationalists,
it meant little: the divers simply hadn't found the weapons yet. Of
course they would have been stowed away deep in the ship's bows,
where the *bakufu* wouldn't find them. They refused to let go of their
dream, even after a second, a third, and a fourth expedition failed to
retrieve any. And while national interest has faded, the dream of the
Tomo Lovers lives on at the *Iroha-maru* Exhibition Hall, capturing
thousands of visitors who yearly cross its threshold with the mystery
of the wreck and the romance of Sakamoto Ryōma's adventures. His

photograph, the image of a handsome young man in traditional Japanese garb with dagger, leaning on a wooden column with his right elbow, his hand nonchalantly slung into the hem of his jacket, and his eyes confidently fixed on a future filled with promise, captivates every new generation. Like a Japanese James Dean, his early death at the hands of an assassin only served to amplify a fame of which any wannabe influencer would be jealous.

Benten Island as seen from the window of the Fukuzen Temple

It so happened that one of the two 'pleasant temples' Kaempfer mentions was the venue of the negotiations between Ryōma and the Kishū representatives. The Fukuzen Temple still exists and can be visited for a modest fee. It is certainly worthwhile to do so, not just because it was visited by Japan's national hero, but also because the view from the temple's Taichōrō reception hall toward nearby Benten Island is captivating.

Shimotsui

After Mitarai and Tomonoura, Shimotsui was a bit of a letdown. With a skyline dominated by the towering Shimotsui-Seto Bridge, there is little to remind the visitor of its former importance as a port, except for the many fishing boats in its concrete harbor and a few remaining Edo-period dwellings. One of them houses the Shimotsui

Shimotsui's alleys, now dominated by the towering Shimotsui-Seto Bridge

Shipping Agent Museum. In a permanent exhibition on the building's second floor, artifacts and images illustrate the port's maritime history, but there was no reminder of the Mission ever having called at the port. It wasn't surprising. Whereas the Dutch did stop over at Mitarai, they left Shimotsui on their larboard side to sail on toward their next port of call, Murotsu. Hence Kaempfer describes the port only in passing:

We weighed anchor by break of day, and having sailed seven sea miles between several small islands, we came to the town of Shimotsui, situated upon the continent of Honshū, upon the rocky coasts of the province of Bitchū, at the foot of a mountain, which has a row of fir trees planted over its top, after the manner of other cultivated mountains, chiefly in the several islands we passed by in our voyage from Shimonoseki. This town consists of four to five hundred houses and is divided into three parts, each governed by a *yoriki* [constable]. Opposite it, on the right hand, stands a castle called Shimotsui, built of freestone, with a neighboring small village.

The Inland Sea at this point is at its narrowest and most heavily sailed, reasons for which, already during the last decade of the 16th century, Ukita Hideie (1572–1655) had the stronghold built to control the traffic and to levy taxes for the upkeep of his domain. It went through various iterations, only to be torn down under the *bakufu*'s Ikkoku Ichijō-*rei* of 1615, under which a lord was allowed only 'one castle per domain' (in this case, that of Okuyama). The 'castle' Kaempfer saw, then, was rather the remains of Shimotsui Castle, something he would have noticed had the Mission landed.

Murotsu

The next port of call for the Mission was Murotsu. For Blomhoff, Fischer, and Siebold, it was also the last. While Kaempfer's Mission disembarked again from Murotsu to sail straight into Osaka, the other three Missions all disembarked at Murotsu and traveled the next 65 miles over land. In doing so, they followed the Saigoku Kaidō, the old high road that skirted the northern shore of the Inland Sea. Neither Fischer nor Siebold explains why their guides decided to travel over land instead of water, but Blomhoff gives us a clue. Still writing in his odd 3rd-person voice, he describes how, having entered the Inland Sea,

> The wind remained contrary, reasons for which they finally let themselves be rowed on the 6th and 7th, each time progressing only a few miles. Yet just as often, hard winds from the north forced them to retreat to Kamuro.
>
> On the 8th of March, the wind grew more favorable, at which occasion they continued their voyage, but only slowly, until (after a pitiable sea journey of thirteen days), on the 15th of March 1818, they arrived in the town of Muro.

The name of Murotsu consists of two Chinese characters, the one meaning 'room,' the other 'haven,' that is to say, the port was well protected and, according to a local topography from the Nara period, 'as quiet as a room.' Kaempfer describes Murotsu (at that time known as Muro) as follows:

> The harbor of Muro is not very spacious, but one of the safest in case of a storm, it being well defended by a mountain which runs out westward from the main continent and covers a great part of it. Going in, ships must steer N.E., then turn S.S. by E. in order to come to an anchor not far from the city. Great part of the harbor is enclosed with a strong wall built of freestone.

The situation of the city is very pleasant and agreeable. It is built along this wall and belongs to the Province of Bizen. It consists of one long narrow street, which runs along the semicircular shores, and some few others, which run backward up towards the mountains. The number of houses may amount in all to about six hundred. It is inhabited chiefly by *sake* brewers, alehouse keepers, and mercers, who can richly maintain themselves because of the multitude of ships, which daily resort to this harbor.

The history of Murotsu as a seaport and a node in the *sankin kōtai* route is on display at the Murotsu Kaieki-*kan*, or the Murotsu Sea Station Hall on the harbor's east quayside. It turned out to be, not so much a hall, but the former abode of a local ship's chandler known as the Shima-*ya*. The misrepresentation was understandable, for the two-story building was huge. In the ground floor exhibition, a large area had been left in the state in which one would have found it during the Edo period, with lots of the kind of utensils used in a ship's chandler's daily life. The *sankin kōtai* system under which the *opperhoofd* was obliged to visit Edo was also on display, but it focused on the Japanese *daimyō* who stayed at the port's six *honjin*. Though the inns have all since gone, a number of their banners—the equivalent of the British pub signs—were still on display at the museum. There was even a small display about the Edo Sanpu.

The *daimyō*s and *opperhoofd*s were not the only dignitaries to pass through Murotsu on their way to the *shōgun*. The rest of the exhibition was related to the so-called Chōsen Tsūshin-*shi*, the diplomatic missions to Japan from the Joseon kingdom on the Korean Peninsula. From 1392 onward, in the course of more than four

92

centuries, more than eighty such missions visited Japan. Led by three envoys—a chief envoy, a vice envoy, and a scribe—they consisted of up to five hundred members and sailed in huge fleets.

Oddly—but perhaps understandably considering the Japanese's obsession with food—a large part of the display was dedicated to the multi-course meals served at the luxurious *honjin*. Tray after tray filled the cabinets with the kind of plastic but highly realistic food

Murotsu's Kaieki-kan

models one might find in the shop window of a modern-day Japanese restaurant, along with detailed menus of what was on offer.

A fixed item of the Dutch Mission's sightseeing tour during its stay at Murotsu was the Kamo Shrine, which still stands on an elevated headland protecting the harbor from southerly winds. The shrine was especially famed for a two-story tower, the Tatama-*tō*, which stood just left of the temple. A scale model of it is on permanent display at the Murotsu Kaieki-*kan*. Siebold, too, visited the shrine:

> We went up to the two-story tower that stood west of the group of chapels on a similarly raised platform. Constructed of wood, it is a true architectural masterpiece. It had only been built recently, and the priests showed us a recently drawn diagram of which we sought to obtain a copy. In this we succeeded, for a year later, we received it along with a drawing of the shrine and a view toward the sea. It would be impossible to describe here in detail the beautiful tower structure. Suffice it to say that such towers are not part of the [Shintō] *kami* worship but the Buddha cult, to wit, they belong to the Shingon sect and were introduced to Japan at the same time as the Buddha cult.

Today, the two-story tower is no more, though its stone foundation is still in place. It is unclear when exactly the tower was removed. It might have been lost through fire. It may also have been dismantled under the same Meiji *shinbutsu bunri* policy that proved the undoing of Shimonoseki's Amida Temple.

.

Saigoku Kaidō

The history of the Saigoku Kaidō is rooted in the Sanyōdō, the ancient land route between the Yamato imperial court and its Dazaifu regional offices in Kyushu. Established during the Asuka period (538–710), the high road ran for three hundred and fifty miles and had fifty-four post stations. They were situated at intervals of roughly seven miles and carefully maintained, each station having some twenty packhorses along with accommodations to spend the night.

During the military period, when the country disintegrated into rivaling states, the high road and its stations fell into disrepair, yet it continued to function as an important traffic artery between the eight western provinces through which it ran—Harima, Mimasaka, Bizen, Bitchū, Bingo, Aki, Suo, and Nagato. And when, during the second half of the 16th century, the warlord Oda Nobunaga launched his campaign to subdue the western provinces, it was largely along the Sanyōdō that his general Hideyoshi moved his vast armies.

It was during the early Edo period, when the Tokugawa bakufu revamped the old post-town system, that the old highway became known as the Saigoku Kaidō or the 'West Countries Highway.' The 'new' high road ran from Kyoto to Shimonosiki, thus connecting the Nagasaki Kaidō to Japan's main traffic arteries of the inland Nakasendō and the coastal Tōkaidō. The number of post towns along the Saigoku Kaidō was reduced by two and the road width was fixed at two-and-a-half kan (just under five yards). The high road's importance only grew when, in 1635, the bakufu called into life the sankin kōtai *system of alternate attendance.*

Himeji

Picking up the Mission's route toward Himeji along the Saigoku Kaidō from the old castle town of Tatsuno made my job a lot easier. I no longer had to whiz around the countless islands of the Inland Sea in hydrofoils—a tough job, admittedly, but someone had to do it. Following the same route two centuries ago, Siebold waxed lyrical:

> We now found ourselves on the great country road and enjoyed a delightful view. The well-maintained road, which, besides cereal and vegetable fields, wound its way through pine forests, hamlets, and village, made us feel as if we were taking a stroll among our native parks. It seemed as if the road had been purposefully designed so that, at every bend, its traveler would be surprised by a new vista. The Japanese are exceptionally fond of beautiful views, and when they design their villas, they are mindful of integrating the surrounding landscape with their garden so as to make them blend into a harmonic whole. At one place, they obscure a jarring contour in the landscape with high cypresses; at another, by a bamboo thicket or an artfully raised hill planted with azaleas and dwarf pines—and all this to make a picturesque mountain, a temple, or a rock overflowing with well water appear in a better light.

However much I wanted to, I found it impossible to share in Siebold's delight with the landscape at this stretch of the Saigoku Kaidō. After the site of the old ferry crossing across the Ibi River, the asphalted highway warily traced its old route through a flat and charmless neighborhood, hemmed in on the left by the viaducts of National Route 2, and on the right by the raised tracks of the Sanyō Shinkansen, which sliced through an already deeply scarred landscape in a cruel and final *coup de grâce*. The Japanese had clearly let go of the ambition to 'integrate the surrounding landscapes with their gardens.' Instead, it now seemed as if everything had been purposefully designed so that, at every twist of the road, its traveler would be

The 'old' Saigoku Kaidō along the raised tracks of the Sanyō Shinkansen

shocked by yet more ugliness. The Japanese who lived here might still love a beautiful view, but amidst the encroaching high roads, railway tracks, parking lots, and high-voltage pylons, they were now forced to limit their scope to the confines of the concrete walls and metal fences behind which they tended to their little gardens.

After all the bleakness of the 'old' high road, the city of Himeji came as a welcome relief. Though a thoroughly modern city, today's

Himeji breathes an atmosphere of prosperity. Its streets were clean and tidy, and unlike other cities I had passed through, most of its shops were still in business. The Saigoku Kaidō, which still enters the city center by crossing the Senba River just west of the castle, passes straight through the city's downtown area. Much of that trajectory consists of a roofed shopping mall, the Nikaimachi Shōtengai, which runs for half a mile and is only interrupted by the

Himeji Castle's magnificent keep as seen from the third bailey

Ōtemae-*dōri*, the wide avenue that connects the northern entrance of Himeji Station to the Sakura Gate Bridge, the entrance to the castle's third bailey.

Much of Himeji's prosperity is down to the tourist attraction of Himeji Castle. It must have been a sign of the ubiquity of Japanese castles during the Edo period that the Mission's members paid so little attention to the castle on their way through. Kaempfer, who

98

dedicated whole paragraphs to Edo Castle, wastes no more than a few lines on Himeji. Blomhoff merely manages to note the presence of a 'handsome castle,' Siebold has more eye for the town than the castle that spawned it, while Fischer ignores it altogether. By the same token, it must be the tragic loss of so many other castles since the Meiji period that, today, Himeji Castle—also known as the Shirasagi-*jō*, or White Heron Castle, because of its white exterior and silver-grey tiles—is Japan's most iconic castle. With its detailed and artful late-Warring-States architecture, it is a paragon of Japanese castle design and has rightfully made it to the list of UNESCO World Heritage Sites.

The castle's origins go back to 1333, when a chieftain named Akamatsu Norimura (1277–1350) chose a local hill by the name of Hime-*yama* to build himself a castle. The castle's first structure was a far cry from the present one: just a wooden palisade with a gate, perhaps a turret, and a cluster of buildings inside. The castle underwent several improvements during the middle of the 16th century, including the addition of tenement houses for lower-ranking samurai and merchants. It was the beginning of Himeji's castle town. The castle itself, however, did not change in essence; it remained a typical mountain stronghold, relying on its elevation for its main protection.

The real transformation of Himeyama Castle came toward the end of the 16th century, when Toyotomi Hideyoshi chose the stronghold as the launchpad from which to pacify western Honshū. Tearing most of the original structures down, he built a three-story keep at the top of the hill, though this time it sat on a solid stone foundation with the gradually slanting slopes so typical of late 16th-century castle design. The palisades made way for plastered walls topped with tiles to keep the mortar from being washed away.

At this time the Saigoku Kaidō still ran north of the castle. Hideyoshi intended Himeji to be the military as well as the commercial center of Harima Province, and thus he redirected the high road to run south of the castle. To facilitate trade he designed a large castle town to provide refuge to merchants who had fled the scene of fighting elsewhere in the region.

The castle's next expansion came in the wake of Tokugawa Ieyasu's victory in the Battle of Sekigahara and the defeat of the western chieftains. Ieyasu granted the stronghold and its domain to Ikeda Terumasa (1565–1613). Not that Terumasa had played any significant role in the battle. But being married to Ieyasu's second daughter, Tokuhime, and as a trusted man among Tokugawa circles, he was just the right man to control the defeated western warlords. Backed by Ieyasu, Terumasa launched a massive project to expand his castle, causing three neighboring villages to be swallowed up. The castle now received its present five-story keep, as well as three minor keeps: an east three-story keep, a northwest three-story keep, and a west three-story keep.

The new Himeji Castle was a stronghold on the scale of Ōsaka, Hiroshima, and Kumamoto. Its many walls were graced by sixty-six turrets, while the raised parapets atop the walls were pierced by close to a thousand arrow loopholes. The castle's most ingenious design aspect was the approach to its keep, which consisted of a long and winding, maze-like succession of steps, gates, and narrow pathways that exposed all who entered to the jealous eyes of watchful guards atop the wall's turrets and raised parapets.

It was only through a string of fortunate happenstances, really, that Himeji Castle was preserved for us to enjoy. In its drive toward modernization, the Meiji government decided to have it demolished. It

100

was sold for just over ¥23 (roughly $1500 in today's money) to Kanbe Seijirō, a wealthy merchant from the castle town's Yoneda quarter. He had intended to sell off the castle's roof tiles to be reused in the town's expansion but soon found them to be too heavy and too costly to remove. Abandoned but untouched, the castle was sold to the military, who stationed its 10th Infantry Regiment within the third bailey. To accommodate them, most of the bailey's structures were dismantled, while a large section of the castle's eastern outer moat was filled up. Eight years later, a fire destroyed all the buildings located within the small bailey called the Bizen-*maru*, immediately in front of the keep.

Luckily, the second half of the 1870s saw a growing call for Himeji Castle to be preserved. By then, the roof structures were beginning to rot, walls were caving in, and the whole castle was overgrown with weeds and ivy. On the initiative of Himeji City's mayor, Asukai Masahisa, a plan was drafted for the castle's restoration, but after much stalling, the military was only able to raise half of the required funds. Eventually, with the support of the local community and a petition to the House of Representatives, the necessary funds were secured. Restorations were begun in 1910, in which most of the castle's main structures, including the main and three minor keeps, were saved from collapse. Following the completion of restoration, the Himeji municipality purchased the sections of the castle that were not being used by the military, and in 1912, the inner citadel and the second and third bailey were opened to the public as Himeyama Park.

The castle again came close to destruction during the Second World War. On 3 July 1945, more than a hundred B-29 bombers from the XXI Bomber Command of the Twentieth Air Force stationed on the Mariana Islands took off to bomb Himeji, Kōchi, Takamatsu, and Tokushima. During the air raid, more than seven hundred tonnes of incendiary bombs were dropped on Himeji alone, destroying two-thirds of the city's built-up area. Though many of the castle's lower structures were badly damaged, its keep miraculously survived the one-hour-long air raid. One incendiary bomb did hit the keep. It crashed through a boarded-up window on the south side of its upper story, which probably absorbed so much of the impact, that the device failed to explode.

The castle's post-war history has been one of continuous revival. Throughout the 1940s, 50s, and 60s, the castle was the scene of large-scale repairs, causing it to be nicknamed the Shōwa Chikujō, or 'Shōwa Castle Construction,' as it covered much of the Shōwa era. The most comprehensive repairs were carried out between 1956 and 1964 when the keep was subjected to an extensive overhaul. It was during these works, in which much of the structure was dismantled, repaired, and reassembled, that a cache of old documents, as well as remnants of the former castle palace within the Bizen-*maru* were discovered. In more recent years, the keep has again been the focus of extensive repair works. The post-war overhaul was projected to keep the structure safe for the next fifty years, but research showed that large sections of the stuccoed walls and parts of the wooden structure had deteriorated beyond expectation. Beginning in 2009, all the walls were repaired and re-plastered with mold-resistant mortar to prevent the typical blackening, while the whole roof was retiled. To do this, the keep was covered by a temporary structure with its own canopy. Today, most of Himeji Castle's structures are listed either as National Treasures or Important Cultural Properties. They include all the keep's structures, twenty-seven turrets, fifteen gates, and most of the remaining walls.

'Temples'

On their way from the castle town of Himeji to the castle town of Akashi, Siebold and other members of the Mission visited three local sites of interest:

> In the afternoon, we continued our earlier planned pilgrimage to the famous Sonenomatsu, the Ishinoden, and Takasago temples. The first one is made famous by the legend that the god Tenjin in person planted a number of fir trees at the shrine; the second by the legend that it was the site where an enormous rock suddenly appeared out of nowhere; the third by a still living fir tree whose branches are spread out like a lime tree, covering an area with a diameter of roughly twenty-eight to thirty feet.

All three 'temples' (they are all shrines) are still there. Sadly, the Sone no Matsu, the giant pine tree (there was just one) at the Sone Tenman Shrine, is gone. Tenjin, alias Sugawara Michizane, who is indeed believed to have visited the temple on his way into exile at the Daizaifu in 901, is said to have planted its seedling with the words 'If I am without sin, then flourish!' It seems the court official was indeed without sin, for the seedling flourished into the mighty pine tree observed by the German physician almost a millennium later. By then, however, it was already dying. It was replaced by a tree that had been grown from a seedling planted a few decades earlier, which kept on growing—and proving Michizane's innocence—until 1952, when it, too, died. Its withered trunk, covered with the scars of weevils and sawyers, is now preserved within a dedicated shrine called the Tamamatsu-*den*, which stands just inside the main gate.

The giant rock at the Ōshiko Shrine, just two miles east of the Sone Tenman Shrine, was also still there. It might have suddenly appeared out of nowhere but it was hard to imagine it would suddenly disappear again. The megalith is just that: enormous. Measuring twenty by nineteen by twenty-four feet, its slender foot sits in a small

The Ishi no Hōden

pond, making it seem as if it floats on the water despite its massive weight, which is estimated at five hundred tons. It sits on the east flank of Mt. Hōden, reasons for which it is known as the Ishi no Hōden. Its front surface is rugged and looks as if it used to be part of a natural, albeit perpendicular cliff face. But at the rear, where it has been carved out of the hill's rock face, it has a giant, wedge-shaped, and perfectly symmetric protrusion, which makes the whole

104

thing look like a vast anvil on which the gods forged their swords. Its flanks, too, have been tooled, with two deep and straight grooves from top to bottom, tricking the modern, technical mind into thinking the whole block is intended to lock into some greater god-like contraption. The overall effect of this remarkable structure is unsettling. The visitor comes away in a state of bewildered awe and confusion as to its true purpose. In that sense, it is truly god-like: it is simply too much for the human mind to contain.

The Takasago Shrine, which sits just west of the nearby Kakogawa River, also still has its spread-out pine tree. Like the old pine tree at the Sone Tenman Shrine, it is not the one Siebold described. That tree was allegedly planted by Honda Tadamasa (1575–1631), the first lord of the Himeji domain. Known as the Aioi no Matsu, or Twin Pine because of its double trunk, it lived well into the 20th century, when it was designated a natural monument by the regional authorities. It was replaced by a new tree that soon fell prey to the same insects that devoured the Sone no Matsu. The present Aioi no Matsu, I was pleased to see, is still going strong.

None of the three 'temples,' however, was worth the while of *Opperhoofd* Johan Willem de Sturler. 'Surly' would have been a more fitting name, for the military man wasn't in the mood for sightseeing and even turned down an invitation to attend a *sumō* match held in his honor. If we can believe Siebold, the man was still smarting from the fire that destroyed his residence on Dejima for a second time since the huge fire more than two decades earlier:

> Our *opperhoofd* did not visit the last three temples and even withdrew himself from the small *sake* party to which the Dutch tend to be treated by a local *sumō* wrestler. He [De

Sturler] had arrived in Nagasaki three months earlier and had invited us to visit him at Dejima. But by the time we did, his residence and all its furniture had been destroyed in a huge fire; and instead of the energetic man we knew, we found a poor friend who dwelled in just a few poor shacks, erected where, according to his description, once stood a stately residence.

By now, however, the patience of the dutiful German had run out with the sulking Dutchman, who turned out to be a bigot and a miser to boot:

It is incomprehensible to me how an envoy of a nation that is treated here with such respect can conduct himself in such an unfriendly manner based on prejudices that are utterly unfounded. In such instances, I have often been seized by feelings of profound shame and have sought to maintain the honor of our Mission by forking out great expenses, being, after all, a representative of a nation whose government earnestly endeavors to display to these Asians a taste of European generosity at each occasion. Yet how is generosity to prevail in our envoy?

Akashi

Like Himeji Castle, Akashi Castle must have been a beautiful sight for all who passed through Akashi. It still is, even though it never received a keep. But nowadays it is dwarfed by the Akashi Kaikyō

Ōhashi, the huge suspension bridge that straddles the Akashi Strait and, together with the Ōnaruto and Konaruto bridges, connects the mainland of Honshū to the islands of Awaji and Shikoku. At 6,532 feet, it had the longest central span in the world when it was completed in 1998. Today, it comes in second after the Çanakkale Bridge across the Dardanelles Strait, which outstretches it by a hundred feet.

Akashi Castle, still a worthy subject for a painting

Next to unfavorable winds, the Akashi Strait was an important reason why the Mission—along with most western *daimyō* on their way to Edo—preferred to disembark at Murotsu and proceed over land along the Saigoku Kaidō. Sitting between the island of Awaji and the main island of Honshū, the strait formed a major obstacle for all traffic between Osaka and the Inland Sea. With a width of just over two miles, yet trafficked by hundreds of *kitamae-bune*, the strait was considered a hazard to steer well clear of. A detour around Awaji Island also wasn't an option. For one, because the island almost spans the width of the Inland Sea, but also because the opposite Narutō Strait was infamous for its eddying currents. Today, the Naruto whirlpools are an attraction for tourists, who can view them from the safety of modern vessels with powerful engines or—even safer—from the Uzunomichi Observatory, an observation deck suspended under the Ōnaruto Bridge. One section of the deck has a floor in which large windows have been mounted for tourists to try and walk on if they dare.

Kaempfer, whose Mission was the only one of the four to pass through the strait, picked up a tale of riches along the way:

> This and some neighboring small Islands were given in former times to some peasants, to be by them and their posterity possessed forever, on condition, that they should improve and cultivate the ground, and pay a small matter by way of a yearly tribute to the lord of the place. These people are now grown so rich, that some of them are possessed of twenty to thirty chests of gold, as they express themselves in this country.

Tough Kaempfer's story sounds like a tall tale told by an old skipper, there might actually be some truth in it, for he might be referring to the Inada, whose name means 'paddy field.' The Inada were a clan of retainers to Lord Hachisuka Yoshishige (1586–1620), who had been granted Awaji Island in reward for his role in Tokugawa Ieyasu's siege of Osaka Castle in 1615. For the young Yoshishige, whose headquarters of Tokushima Castle stood on the eastern tip of Shikoku, the gift posed more of a burden than a blessing. He was

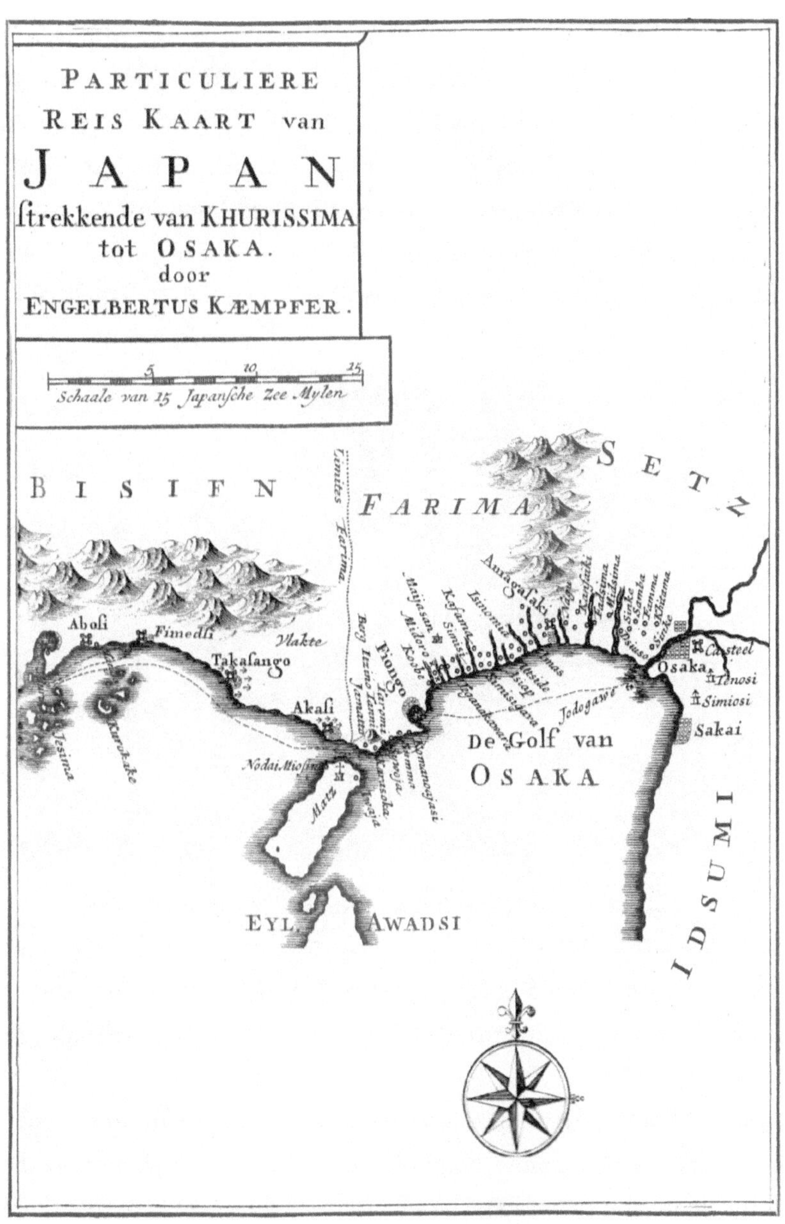

From Akō to Osaka

already in the midst of difficult land reforms at home to produce more indigo, a dye that was in high demand at that time. Now, all of a sudden, he found himself in charge of another large domain. Suffering from poor health (he would die at the age of thirty-four) and already taxed with the management of his Tokushima domain, he turned to his Inada retainers, from whose ranks he had drawn many of his elders. And so it was that, from then onward, the Inada-

The Akashi Strait Bridge, gateway to Awaji Island

karō, the 'Paddy Feld elders,' governed Awaji Island. They did so from their new headquarters of Sumoto Castle, on the island's east shore.

Siebold, who had to make do with a view of the island from across the strait, seemed almost disappointed at not being able to enjoy the strait from the water. Yet he still managed to take delight in the scenery:

The strait between this island and the island of Nippon is one Japanese *ri* wide. The waterway seemed deep enough, and we saw the Japanese barks tacking to and fro in all directions. We enjoyed a wonderful view of the sea at the village of Maiko no Hama, in the vicinity of which I made some observations using my sea compass.

Kōbe

The closer I got to densely urbanized Kōbe and Osaka, the harder it became to detect some of the old Japan. The beach at Maiko, with its beautiful backdrop of Awaji Island, was gone. Now there was a concrete promenade from where one could marvel at the engineering feat of the Akashi Strait Ōhashi.

It was not much different at Suma no Hama, once a picturesque beach with pine trees and a few sails in the offing. There was still a beach (behind a fenced tarmac promenade), but now, one had to cough up ¥1.800 to enter. Those who paid their dues gained access to a designated plot of a dozen square feet, each rigorously demarcated by a little red flag. For the Japanese—for whom the sea officially 'opens' in May and 'closes' in September—it might all make sense but to me, it was just depressing.

The Kōbe Bay Cruise aboard the Royal Princess against the musical backdrop of Clayderman-like elevator music only went so far to lift my spirits. The beautiful colonial-style Oriental Hotel had long since gone. Now one was left to admire the Kōbe Meriken Park Oriental, a pyramid-shaped monstrosity that caters to well-to-do pensioners who just as happily disembark from their giant cruise ships at places like Dubai or Qatar. Modern-day Kōbe's harbor front differs little from such places: if one wouldn't know any better, one might be led to think its skyscrapers and palm trees had sprung from a barren desert.

I arrived at the Minato Hutte, the inn I had booked in Kōbe for the night, together with another foreigner. The inn was closed, but a notice said guests should check in at the back entrance. The back

Modern-day Kōbe

entrance, too, was locked, but there was a lock that you could open with a cipher combination. The trouble was that I didn't have any code; the confirmation email they had sent me didn't mention one. The other foreigner hadn't received one either. I fumbled with the lock but it wouldn't budge. Then there was some stumbling inside, the door swung open, and an apologetic owner let us in.

Sharing our relief at not having to spend the night on the street, the other foreigner and I introduced ourselves and, while the owner checked us in, we started chatting. Yossel was a German of Jewish descent. He was on a six-month tour through Asia and was now doing bits of Japan. He was especially looking forward to visiting Takayama with its traditional woodworking industry. Like me, he wasn't very keen on Kōbe. Then why come? The sole reason for his visit, he explained, was that, as a practicing Jew, he wanted to observe the Shavuot, or the 'feast of weeks,' celebrating the revelation of the Torah on Mt. Sinai to the Jewish people. And it so happened that, next to Osaka, Kōbe was the only city in Japan with a Synagogue. Yossel's family was originally from Ukraine. They had fled eastward before the German onslaught of the Second World War. After the war, his grandmother, an electrician, had been forcefully migrated to Latvia. His mother had finally moved to Germany.

I was fascinated by Yossel's family history, but he was in a hurry. He still had to find a barber before he could attend the ceremony. And so, after a short siesta, I strolled up to Kōbe's Kitano Ijinkan-*gai*, or 'Foreign Residences Road.' It is related to Kōbe's late-19th-century Gaikokujin Kyoryū-*chi*, or Foreign Settlement. Opened up to foreign trade under the 1858 Treaty of Amity and Commerce between Japan and the United States, Kōbe saw a great influx of foreign settlers. To house them the Japanese authorities conceded a wide stretch of land in front of the port to the foreign powers. Spanning some 25 hectares, its borders were demarcated by the Koi River to the west, the Saigoku Kaidō to the north, and the Ikuta River to the east. Its main avenue was the Kaigan-*dōri*, or the 'Coast Street,' better known as The Bund among the port's foreign settlers.

The Kitano Ijinkan-*gai* only came about at the turn of the 20th century, after the Japanese had managed to negotiate the return of the foreign settlements and Japanese companies like Mitsui and Osaka Merchant Shipping were able to open offices on the Bund in large buildings designed by prestigious architects. At the same time, many foreign residents chose to relocate to the pleasant surroundings of Kōbe's Kitano Township, which sits on the slope of the hills north of Kōbe and was still only a half-hour's stroll away from The Bund and the downtown foreign offices and businesses.

Kōbe's Kitano Ijinkan-gai

The area got its name from the Kitano Tenman Shrine, which stands at the foot of Mt. Dōtoku. It was founded in 1180 by Taira no Kiyomori when he moved the capital to nearby Fukuhara-*kyō*. The move wasn't popular among the members of the imperial court, who complained about the area's rainy climate. Within six months the court had moved back to Kyoto. But the shrine remained and still graces the northern outskirts of the eponymous township.

Kinai

The Kinai is the central region of Japan that covers the densely urbanized area stretching from Kōbe, through Osaka, to Kyoto. The term 'kinai' is Chinese in origin and refers to an area within 125 miles from the imperial court. When the term was introduced into Japan, the imperial court stood in central Yamato Province (today's Nara Prefecture). Apart from Yamato, the provinces that fell within that radius were Yamashiro, Settsu, Kawachi, and Izumi. As the ancient center of Japanese civilization, the Kinai area is incredibly rich in history and has by far the country's greatest density of national treasures. It is also the most populated area after the Kantō region around Tokyo. As such, it still presents a softer, more cultured counterweight to the hard-nosed political power of the capital.

During the Meiji period, the term Kinki, or the 'area near the capital,' came into fashion. But in more recent years, the term's embarrassing similarity to the English word 'kinky,' has caused it to fall out of favor again, and reputable institutes like Kinki University and Kinki Nippon Railway have quietly changed their names to Kindai University and Kintetsu Railway. Though the area has never been strictly defined and has no legal foundation, the general consensus is that it covers the prefectures of Kyoto, Osaka, Nara, Wakayama, Hyōgo, Mie, and Shiga.

Today, the area is more popularly known (and publicly promoted) as the Kansai-chihō, or the Kansai region. Despite its modern connotations, the term itself is again a throwback to ancient times, for it refers to the region 'west of the barrier,' the ancient toll gate that guarded the capital from the country's inhospitable and barbarous eastern regions.

Osaka

Kaempfer's Mission was the only one among the four to sail past the
Akashi Strait and enter Osaka by boat:

> Having made today ten miles, we got as far as the mouth of
> the Yodo River, and about eleven in the forenoon entered its
> navigable arm, steering E.S.E. We were received here by our
> landlord, who conducted us up the river in two stately boats.
> We passed by several new villages and small towns, or rather
> suburbs of Osaka, which had been built along the banks of
> this river for these several years last past, and amidst upwards
> of a thousand boats we entered the city itself, which is
> separated from the suburbs by two strong stately guardhouses,
> one on each side of the river. Having passed under six fine
> wooden bridges, we had leave at last to go on shore, and
> having walked up some stone steps, we turned into a narrow
> street, through which we were led to our inn, which lies at
> one of the corners facing the great street, where we arrived
> between one and two of the clock in the afternoon.

It is hard to ascertain where exactly the members of the various
Missions were lodged during their stay in Osaka as hardly any of the
structures of the time remain. But one thing is clear, the lodgings
were a thoroughly humble affair. To Kaempfer, it 'would have been
commodious enough, if we had not been very much incommoded
by the smoke, they knowing nothing in this country of chimneys.'
Blomhoff finds the accommodations 'not very attractive,' and even
the generally positive Siebold describes them as the worst of the

whole journey. Perhaps in jest, they were known by the Dutch as the Keizerlijke Geldkamer or the Emperor's Money Room, the reason being that it was run by the Tamegawa family, whose heads were in charge of the local Tokugawa Mint.

Fisher mentions how, on their way to their lodgings, the Mission's members drew a lot of attention:

> The streets were crowded with the curious, to such an extent that the police were only able to maintain order with utmost difficulty. One would have gladly made one's entry into town on foot, yet given the commotion, we had to remain within our *norimono*, so that we saw only little of the manifold and beautiful shops.

Much of what Kaempfer observed about Osaka more than three centuries ago still rings true today:

> Osaka is extremely populous, and, if we believe what the boasting Japanese tell us, can raise an army of 80.000 men, only from among its inhabitants. It is the best trading town in Japan, being extraordinarily well situated for carrying on commerce both by land and water. This is the reason why it is so well inhabited by rich merchants, artificers, and manufacturers.

Having reached Osaka by land like the other three Missions, I made my way into the city across the Tenjin Bridge. I began to follow the west bank of the Higashi Yokobori-*gawa*, the old moat that used to form Osaka Castle's westernmost defense. Already in Kaempfer's day, the moat was straddled by a large number of bridges that connected the Uemachi district west of the castle's outer bailey to the commercial district of Senba. All except one of the bridges were set on fire during the siege. They were all rebuilt in its wake and were still there when Siebold visited Osaka in 1826 and counted (possibly on one of his illegal maps) more than a hundred and fifty bridges in all of Osaka.

At that time, the best-known bridge across the west moat was the Kōrai-*bashi*. Like Tokyo's Nihonbashi Bridge, it formed the node in a network of high roads that included the Saigoku Kaidō toward Himeji, The Kyō Kaidō toward Kyoto, the Kuragari-*goe* Nara Kaidō toward Nara, and the Kishū Kaidō toward Wakayama. The bridge was erected by Toyotomi Hideyoshi when he built his castle in the 1580s. He named it Kōrai after the Goryeo kingdom to placate a Korean embassy that visited the castle on the eve of his second invasion of the peninsula. The original wooden bridge has been immortalized in numerous wood prints and its cast iron successor on photographic plate.

The cast iron version was designed by Motoki Shōzō (1824–75). Shōzō was born into a family of Dutch interpreters in Nagasaki. In the course of his Dutch studies, he developed a deep interest in Western engineering, in particular shipbuilding and steel manufacture. That interest led him to get involved in printing, which in turn led him to begin research on movable type at the local steelworks of the Nagasa Seitetsu-*sho*. To learn more, he invited the Shanghai-based Presbyterian minister William Dill Gamble (1830–68) to Nagasaki, and using Gamble's method of producing metal printing plates by means of electrotyping, the two men eventually managed to develop Japanese movable type. It was such a success

118

that Motoki was able to open a branch office in Osaka in 1870. The Osaka Kappan-*sho*, or the Osaka Print Shop, was located on the city's Ōte-*dōri*, the avenue that runs from the Higashi Yokobori-*gawa* to the Ōte-*mon*, the castle's western main gate.

It was shortly after his arrival in Osaka that Motoki was approached to design a new bridge, which was erected in 1870 and stood until 1929, when it was replaced by the current steel-reinforced concrete

Motoki Shōzō's cast iron Kōrai Bridge, also known as the Kurogane-bashi

bridge. The bridge itself is graceful enough but it still has a hard time standing out from all the concrete and steel around it. In an effort to liven up the area, the west bank of the concrete-clad moat has been turned into the Higashiyokoborigawa Ryokuchi Park, a green zone that stretches from the Imabashi Bridge to the Honmachi Bridge. But it seems the Osakans aren't too keen on having to face their monuments to progress. The park felt neglected, and large stretches were closed off to the public with the kind of rusty fences that look more at home on an abandoned industrial plot.

Little else besides Osaka's moats allows the historically inclined visitor to get a bearing on the layout of the city during the Edo period. This is not helped by the Japanese tendency to view rivers and moats as the perfect playground for raised expressways. Along with the Kōrai Bridge, much of the Higashi Yokobori-*gawa* is

Today's steel-reinforced Kōrai Bridge

obscured by the raised Hanshin Expressway No 1. Perhaps out of respect for their old moat, Osaka's town planners managed to move its northern pylons toward the east bank of the moat, sparing its bridges the same fate as Tokyo's Nihonbashi Bridge.

Things really got crowded as I approached Higashisenba Junction where, in a three-story infrastructural orgy, the Hanshin Expressway No 1 unites with the Hanshin Expressway No 13. The irony of that

120

Higashisenba Junction, a three–story infrastructural orgy

last number will be lost on the Japanese, to whom 4 and 9 are considered unlucky numbers.

I was on my way to Dōton-*bori*, Osaka's most popular night-time entertainment area, a place where attractive young women and men on vast LCD displays promote the latest fads, and where huge suspended figures of blowfish and crabs entice locals and tourists alike to live up to the city's informal creed of *kuidaore*: 'eat till you drop.'

Dōten-bori's famous Ebisu Bridge

The name Dōton-*bori* refers to the old waterway along which all the entertainment is situated. It was named after Yasui Dōton (1533–1615), one of four local entrepreneurs who together hatched a plan to connect the Higashi Yokobori-*gawa* to the Kizu River and turn Senba into an island onto itself. The main aim was to improve access over water to the area and thereby promote its commerce. Hygiene, too, was a consideration. The then moat simply terminated in a dead end toward the south; and this while many of the city's open sewers disgorged their waste right into the moat, turning it into an infernal cesspit that gave off such a foul odor in summer that it made life in the southern reaches of Uemachi and Senba unbearable.

The project was begun in 1612, when all but the most western section of the moat was excavated. Work ground to a halt during the siege and was resumed shortly afterward, not by Dōton, who

*Dōton-*bori *at night*

had been killed during the siege, but by his fellow entrepreneurs, who named the moat after him when it was completed late in 1615.

It was Dōton's fellow entrepreneurs, too, who laid the groundwork for the area's entertainment scene when, to promote trade through the moat, they moved the theaters from nearby Nanba to the south bank of Dōton-*bori*. In many cases, the term 'theater' was a bit of a misnomer. The main form of staged popular entertainment at the time was *kabuki,* comic playlets about everyday life. The roles were initially played by women, who played both female and male roles. The ribaldry and sexual innuendo of these plays attracted huge crowds, especially since many 'actresses' made a handsome living on the side by playing more intimate roles. As a result, their art was also known as *yūjo kabuki,* or 'prostitute *kabuki.*' It was banned by the authorities in 1629. After that, all roles had to be played by men. They, too, didn't shy away from a bit of action on the side so that, in 1652, *wakashū kabuki,* or 'teenage *kabuki,*' was also outlawed. After that, just a few officially recognized theaters were allowed to operate at Dōton-*bori:* the Asahi-*za,* the Benten-*za,* the Kazo-*za,* the Naka-*za,* and the Naniwa-*za.* They were collectively known as the Go-*za,* or the Five Theaters. The *kabuki* and *ningyō jōruri* (puppet) performances staged at the Go-*za* were advertised on large banners attached to so-called *yagura,* or 'turrets,' that were erected over their entrances, reasons for which they were also known as the Go-*yagura.* Not one of the Go-*za* has survived: some were sold off, some were turned into movie theaters, one burned down while being dismantled.

But Doton-*bori* has survived, and it makes it known to the world in true Osaka style: loud, gaudy, in your face. The noise, the flashing lights, and the somewhat obstreperous Osakans, however, have a charm of their own, especially to the young, who at night flock to the area in their thousands, like moths to a flame. If they survive a solid *kuidaore,* they can still go and see a play, for new theaters have sprung up on the moat's south bank, among them the Osaka Chōchiku-*za,* the Dōtembori Zaza, and the Nanba Milulari.

Having survived the onslaught of Dōton-*bori,* I decided to follow the green, temple-studded belt along the city's spine, starting at the

124

Ikutama Shrine and terminating at Tennoji Park, close to which I had booked a hostel for the night. It was along this elevated ridge that, in the summer of 1615, young Lord Toyotomi Hideyori's forces withdrew to his castle after they had been routed at Tennōji by the forces of *Shōgun* Tokugawa Ieyasu. Amid the trees, temples, and shrines, I could breathe again. I was surprised at how peaceful it could be just a ten-minute walk away from the crushing din of Dōton-*bori*.

Tennōji Park, once the scene of fierce fighting

Neither Kaempfer, Blomhoff, Siebold, nor Fischer mentions that Osaka was the place where Ieyasu crossed his Rubicon for the second time (the first time being at Sekigahara). This is surprising. Especially Kaempfer, who visited Osaka just eight decades after it had witnessed the largest battle in the country's history, might have mentioned the siege, for he takes great interest in the stronghold that was at its center:

On the east side of the city, or rather at its northeast extremity, lies the famous castle in a large plain. Going up to Kyoto, we pass by it. It has been built by *Taikō* Toyotomi Hideyoshi. It is square, about an hour's walking in circumference, and strongly fortified with round bastions, according to the military architecture of the country. After Kumamoto Castle, it has not its superior in extent, magnificence, and strength throughout the whole empire. On the north side, it is defended by the Yodo River, which washes its walls, after it has received two other rivers. And though the united stream was of itself of a very considerable breadth, yet for a still greater security they have thought it necessary to enlarge its bed still farther. On the east side, its walls are washed by the Kashiwara River, before it falls into the great arm of the Yodo River. Beyond the Kashiwara River, opposite the castle, lies the great garden belonging to the same. The south and west ends border upon the extremities of the city. The moles, or buttresses, which support the outward wall, are of an uncommon bigness, and I believe at least seven fathoms thick. They are built to support a high strong brick wall, lined with freestone, which at its upper end is planted with a row of firs, or cedars. I took notice that there was a small narrow gate just in the middle of two sides, with a small bridge leading to them.

But not a word about the castle's siege. Might it be that he was not aware? The Japanese were certainly secretive about anything military, something Siebold later found out to his detriment when he was caught in possession of military-grade maps. Thus the foreigners were not allowed to enter the stronghold, and Kaempfer was left

126

describing the layout of the castle based on what he learned from an insider, albeit one very well-informed. The curfew imposed on the foreigners was so strict that, on his departure, Siebold was left likening his stay in Osaka to an incarceration.

Yodo River

Kaempfer's words also still ring true when he describes the scenery as, on its departure, the Mission began to follow the south bank of the Yodo River toward Kyoto:

> The country hereabouts is extraordinary well inhabited, and the many villages along the road are so near one another, that there wants little towards making it one continued street from Osaka quite up to Kyoto.

The scientifically inclined Siebold had more eye for the river, its maritime function, as well as the natural danger it posed:

> The Yodo River is of great importance to trade. Yet since this river is connected to Biwakō, the large lake near Kyoto, it often happens that it causes large floods, which are all the more devastating in that the fields on the left bank lie considerably lower than the river itself.

It was to help address these problems that, half a century later, the Dutch civil engineer Johannis de Rijke (1842–1913) was contracted to help tame the river. He had already worked on a large number of

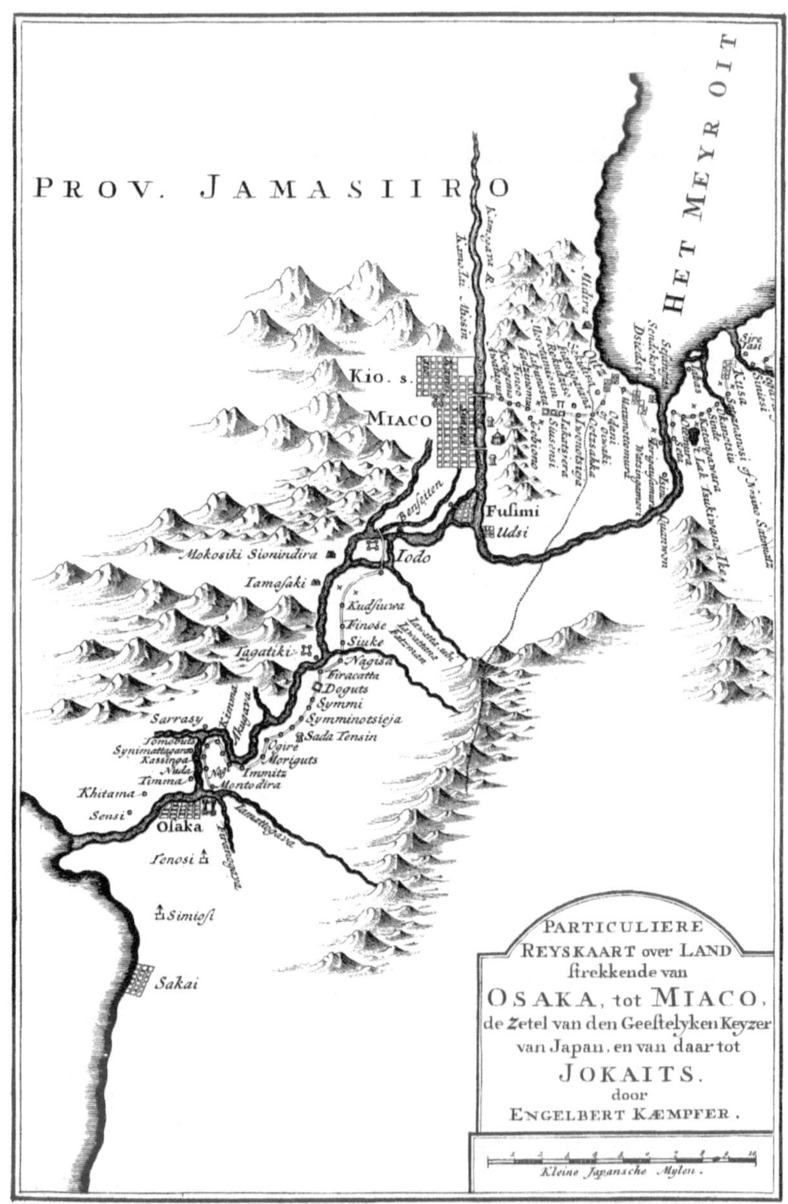

The road from Osaka to Kyoto along the Yodo River

similar projects throughout Japan, helping to improve access to the ports of Yokohama, Nagasaki, and Hakata. But tackling the Yodo River proved his most challenging project.

Assisted by his colleague George Arnold Escher (father of the famed graphic artist), De Rijke drew up a comprehensive plan to canalize the river. The plan even envisioned the construction of a seaport in the river's estuary. Work was begun in 1884, and for the next decade, the two men diligently worked toward the plan's completion. A particularly thorny problem was the huge amounts of sand from eroding mountain slopes that washed down into the river from its many tributaries. Using tested Dutch methods of water management, they eventually succeeded in making the Yodo River more navigable and protecting the surrounding area from flooding, whilst still allowing for its irrigation.

Yodo

A town that took its name from the mighty river was Yodo. In fact, the town did not directly take its name from the river but from Yodo Castle, which in turn was named after the river. The town might just as well have been called Katsura, Uji, or Izu, for the castle and its castle town stood on an island in the confluence of those historic three rivers, just before they merged into the mighty Yodo River, as noted by Kaempfer on his entry into Yodo:

> The small but famous city of Yodo is entirely enclosed with water, and has besides several canals cut through the town, all derived from the arms of the river which encompasses it. The

suburbs consist of one long street, across which we rode to a stately wooden bridge, called Yodo Ōhashi, which is four hundred paces long, and supported by forty arches, to which answer so many banisters, adorned at the upper end with brass-buttons, the whole making an extraordinary good figure. At the end of this bridge is a single well-guarded gate, through which we entered the city.

Yodo Castle as seen through the pylons of the Keehan Railway Line

Today, the castle town of Yodo, like most other towns and villages through which the Mission passed on its way to Kyoto, has been swallowed up by the urban sprawl that has filled the Yodo Delta to its farthest reaches. No trace remains of the stately bridge mentioned by Kaempfer, except for a steel and concrete structure that still carries its name. Only the ruins of what was once Yodo Castle remind the visitor that Yodo was once an important castle town. Once the stronghold had proudly guarded the confluence of the Katsura, Uji, and Kizu rivers; now its former grounds serve as a children's playground while its few remaining walls valiantly try to hold their own between an abandoned factory, a car park, and a forest of concrete pylons of the Keehan Railway Line.

Fushimi

What is true for Yodo applies in almost equal measure to Fushimi, albeit that it has almost retained its name, as it is now known as Kyoto's Fushimi Ward. Indeed, already in Kaempfer's day, Fushimi was considered part of the capital:

> The middle and chief street of Fushimi reaches as far as Kyoto, and is contiguous to the streets of that capital and residence of the Emperor of Japan, insomuch that Fushimi might be called the suburbs of Kyoto, the rather since this last city is not at all enclosed with walls, but lies open towards the fields.

Unlike Yodo, Fushimi's castle has been restored, though nowhere near its former glory; the modern reconstruction is a leftover of Fushimi Momoyama Castle Land, a sad attempt at the one-time splendor of Hideyoshi's original stronghold. It was set up during the roaring sixties for the princely sum of $6 million. Four decades of financial struggles later, it went belly-up. It is now a sports ground. The mockup castle remains, but earthquake tests declared its structures—a ferro-cement main and secondary keep—unsafe for use, and both are now closed to the public. Though still in a better shape than

Yodo Castle, it just sits there, its paint peeling, its walls invaded by ivy, its gravel paths covered in weeds. And yet, its very abandonment lends the place an eerily quiet quality.

Tectonic troubles plagued the stronghold from the very start. In 1596, even while Hideyoshi was personally conducting the stronghold's vast construction project, the area was struck by an earthquake. It destroyed most of the castle's turrets, the palace, as

Fushimi Castle, an eerily quiet place

well as the top two stories of the keep. The quake was so strong that, in nearby Kyoto, the Tō, the Daikaku, and Tenryū temples, the Nison Monastery, and the Daibutsu-*den* of the Hōkō Temple were all flattened. Hideyoshi escaped unharmed, but some six hundred of his twenty thousand laborers, as well as a thousand Kyotoites, were killed. The damage was so extensive, that the *taikō* had to sleep in the castle's kitchen for the next few weeks.

132

By the time Kaempfer passed through Fushimi, there was no stronghold to detect. Hideyoshi's castle, though completed in 1597, had again been destroyed in the run-up to the great Battle of Sekigahara. Its victor, Tokugawa Ieyasu, rebuilt the stronghold, and for a while, he used it when attending functions in the Kinai region. That role was eventually subsumed by Kyoto's Nijō Castle, which received Fushimi's keep. The remaining turrets and buildings were reused at castles throughout the country: at Amagasaki, at Akashi, at Fukuyama, at Yodo, and even at far-away Edo Castle. As a reminder of their origin, these structures often carry the name of Fushimi. Thus the castles of Edo, Ōsaka, and Fukuyama all possess a Fushimi-*yagura*. The moats, too, were filled in and the castle grounds turned into a large orchard of peach trees, thus lending it its local name of Momoyama (Peach Tree Hill).

Kaempfer happened to pass through Fushimi on 28 February 1691, which, according to the lunisolar calendar, coincided with the first day of the second month in the fourth year of the Genroku era:

It was today *tsuitachi* with the Japanese, being the first day of the month, which they keep as a Sunday, or holiday, visiting the temples, walking into the fields, and following all manner of diversions. Accordingly, we found this long street, along which we rode, for full four hours before we got to our inn, crowded with multitudes of the inhabitants of Kyoto, walking out of the city to take the air, and to visit the neighboring temples. Particularly the women were all on this occasion richly appareled in variously colored gowns, according to the fashion of Kyoto, wearing a purple-colored silk about the forehead, and large straw hats to defend themselves from the heat of the sun.

We likewise met some particular sorts of beggars, comically clad, and some masked in a very ridiculous manner, not a few walked upon iron stilts, others carried large pots with green trees upon their heads; some were singing, some whistling, some fluting, others beating bells. All along the street we saw multitudes of open shops, jugglers and players diverting the crowd. The temples, which we had on our right, as we went up, being built in the ascent of the neighboring green hills, were illuminated with many lamps, and the priests beating some bells with iron hammers made such a noise, as could be heard at a considerable distance. I took notice of a large white dog, perhaps made of plaster, which stood upon an altar on our left, in a neatly adorned chapel, or small temple, which was consecrated to the patron of the dogs.

Kyoto

Since the Mission's members were able to explore Kyoto at length, I booked three nights in the former capital for myself, not only to see the sights but also to out-weather typhoon Mawar or, in Japanese parlance, typhoon Nr. 2 (of the season).

One of the sights mentioned by Kaempfer is Mt. Hiei, the site of the famous Enryaku Temple, home of the Tendai sect of Buddhism. Though peaceful today, Mt. Hiei once was the scene of incredible carnage. Kaempfer explains why:

The situation, but much more the sanctity of this mountain, made it a sanctuary and place of refuge for the inhabitants of

Kyoto in the civil wars, which desolated that city. But Oda Nobunanga, ruler of Japan, and predecessor of the great *Taikō* Toyotomi Hideyoshi, out of a general hatred he bore to all priests and monks, as well as to revenge some particular insults he received from those who inhabited this famous mountain, invaded and conquered it at the head of a numerous army, consumed and destroyed all its temples and religious buildings, and cruelly butchered all that vermin of priests, as he called them, with all the other inhabitants.

It would be a grave mistake to think that all those who dwelled on Mt. Hiei were piece-loving monks whose only interest was to recite their daily *nenbutsu* and count the beads on their rosaries. Far from it. Mt. Hiei in Nobunaga's time was a veritable fortress, manned by thousands of fearsome *sōhei*, or 'warrior monks,' who defended the interests of their sect and its vast possessions tooth and nail. As such, these bastions of Buddhist power—on Mt. Hiei near the capital, on Mt. Kōya at the heart of the Ise Penninsula, at the Ishiyama Hongan-*ji* in the mouth of the Yodo River (the site of Osaka Castle), and on Nagashima Island in the delta of the Kiso River—represented a huge challenge to Nobunaga's aim of pacifying the realm. The death of his older brother at the hands of the Tendai monks did little to lessen his resolve to root out the sects once and for all.

I took the cable cart up to the halfway station toward the mountain's summit. At 841 m it was more than my legs and back could bear, as I still had to do the Tōkaidō, the longest stretch over land in my journey. Besides, I knew I would never be able to outclass the marathon monks of Mt. Hiei, who in their one hundred days of

135

meditative running among these same steep slopes, clock up a ten-fold distance of my entire journey.

Despite Nobunaga's act of wanton destruction, the temples that today grace the mount's three crests aren't all latter-day reconstructions. One small structure survived: the Ruri-*dō*, which is part of the temple's Western Pagoda and stands on the northern reach of Mt. Hiei's crest, well away from the main temple, survived the

*The Ruri-*dō*, the one structure that survived Nobunaga's onslaught*

conflagration; and many of the other temples that now grace the mountain were moved there or rebuilt under Nobunaga's successors. Thus the Western Pagoda's Shaka-*dō*, Jōgyō-*dō*, and Hokke-*dō* were rebuilt by Toyotomi Hideyoshi, while the Eastern Pagoda's Konpon Chū-*dō* was rebuilt by Tokugawa Iemitsu.

In 2006, the temple complex again ran afoul of the authorities when it hosted a large ceremony to mourn the souls of successive bosses of the Yamaguchi-*gumi*, Japan's largest *yakuza* organization and, according to some, the largest crime syndicate in the world. Already prior to the ceremony, Kyoto's police urged the temple's abbot to call the whole thing off, rightfully arguing that such events were used by gangs to raise funds. But the abbot argued it was 'just your regular Buddhist service.' And so, on April 21, more than a hundred *yakuza* bigwigs descended on—or should one say, ascended—the

*The Enryaku Temple's Shaka-*dō

mount to commemorate their beloved leaders. The event caused an outcry of indignation, not only among politicians and rivaling *yakuza* gangs, but also among other Buddhist sects. In the end, the scandal was only resolved when the temple's entire senior clergy resigned after they had written an email of apology to some three thousand Buddhist temples nationwide. Clearly, the temple's belligerent strains ran deep.

It was a Sunday, and as I walked back along the west embankment of the Kamo River toward my hostel, it seemed all of Kyoto's inhabitants were at play on and around their river: infants rummaging in the reeds, older children hopping from stone to stone toward the other side, teenagers practicing the choreography from their favorite pop band, aunties striding along with Nordic walking sticks, and an old man feeding a pidgin. All was well with the world.

The west bank of the Kamo River on a quiet day

The next day, I was making my way toward Nijō Castle along Ōmiya Street when, a hundred yards short of my destination, I passed an old house called the Nijō-*jinya*. It was marked by one of those traditional wooden signposts with a little roof. My interest piqued, I read its text:

This was the residence of Senbashi, the oldest son of Ogawa

138

Tosa no Kami Suketada (1535–1601), a vassal of Toyotomi Hideyoshi and the lord of Imabari Castle and a domain of 70.000 *koku*, who took the tonsure following his defeat in the Battle of Sekigahara. Assuming the name of Yokozuya Heiemon, Senbashi moved to this area from where he ran a rice shop, a money exchange, and a tree pharmacy. This building was erected in the tenth year of the Kanbun era (1670) and served as his main residence.

This building later served as a *jinya* for petty and medium *daimyō* who attended on Nijō Castle and Kyoto's *shoshidai*, and it served as the official lodgings of Kyoto's *machi-bugyō*. Equipped with characteristic structures like hidden stories and the like, as well as being built in a fire-proof way, it served to ensure a *daimyō*'s personal safety.

The first part of the text was clearly baloney. Ogawa Suketada wasn't defeated but saved his skin by changing sides. Also, he never had a son by the name of Senbashi. It was one of those many instances where rich merchants wanted to add prestige to their business by claiming they were of noble descent.

But there was no reason to doubt the second paragraph (the building had not been designated an Important Cultural Property for nothing). Such structures were indeed used by *daimyō*, not only during their stay in the capital but also when, under the Ikkoku Ichijō-*rei* mentioned earlier, they weren't allowed to maintain a castle. They were called *jinya*, or 'manor houses.' They offered more protection than a regular *yashiki*, or 'samurai residence,' in that they had no outward-facing windows but only thick stuccoed walls and a heavy gate.

Could it just be that a Dutch Mission stayed here on at least one of their visits to the capital? After all, the *opperhoofd* enjoyed the status of a petty *daimyō*. Moreover, the Dutch, too, had to visit both the *shoshidai* and the *machi-bugyō*, whose offices were located on the opposite, north side of the castle, less than a mile's walk from the Nijō-*jinya*. Housing the foreigners in a *jinya*, furthermore, would have helped to ensure their safety, especially toward the end of the

The Nijō-jinya. Could the Mission have stayed here?

Edo period, when anti-foreign sentiments ran high. Yes, I was inclined to give the Nijō-*jinya* the benefit of the doubt. As for my own safety, typhoon Mawar had passed over, and I was good to start on the last leg of my journey.

Tōkaidō

The Tōkaidō is Japan's best-traveled and best-known highway. It is also the oldest and features in many historical records. In the Sarashina nikki, for instance, a diary written during the late Heian period. In it, the daughter of Sugawara no Takasuke (sadly, we don't know her name) describes her journey through a pristine, utterly enchanting realm as she and her family make their way back to Kyoto after her father's term in office has expired. Setting out from the local government Kokufu offices in Kazusa (Chiba city near Tokyo), they cross the Sumida-gawa, a river along which today live some thirty-six million people:

> *We crossed the river and entered the province of Musashi. The Nishitomi mountain range stretched before us like a huge folding screen decorated with the most splendid paintings. Toward one side lay a wide beach onto which waves broke and retreated as if baring a deeper meaning. At Morokoshigahara, it took us two or three days to cross the blinding white sands.*

Rivers, incidentally, made the Tōkaidō a perilous road to travel. Its travelers had to cross at least a dozen mighty rivers whose waters swelled to fearsome torrents in times of rain. It was only with the establishment of a well-organized system of river-crossing crews that the high road became less dangerous. These crews manned flat-bottomed, shallow-drafted boats, whose floorboards were tough and pliable so that the boats could be slid across a river's pebbled shallows when its waters ran low.

Ōtsu

The first post town along the Tōkaidō from Kyoto was Ōtsu. Having left behind the pleasant comfort of the Hana Hostel in Kyoto's Shimogyō Ward at the break of dawn, I reached Ōtsu well before most shops had opened; with the exception of a talkative local walking his aging German shepherd dog, the town seemed fast

Mii-dera's Gon-dō

asleep. Thankfully, the local Lawson was already open. Grabbing myself a freshly-made *latte macchiato*, I made my way to the Mii-*dera*, a temple mentioned by Kaempfer when he passed through Ōtsu. Actually, he doesn't so much mention the temple but rather a tiny shrine, the Komano Gongen-*sha*, which stands on its northern periphery, just behind the towering roof of the Gon-*dō*, the Golden Hall, which is now a National Treasure. Just why he should mention

142

the tiny shrine and not the temple seems a mystery. He certainly couldn't have overlooked the temple since already in his day its grounds were vast and home to any number of buildings that outsized the shrine by many times. It also seems remarkable that the temple, which is officially known as the Onjō Temple, should have survived Oda Nobunaga's attack on the Enryaku Temple complex atop Mt. Hiei, at which foot the Mii Temple sits, especially since both temples

Mii-dera's wide avenue

belonged to the Tendai sect. Yet for some reason, the warlord was on good terms with the temple's abbot, who even invited him to set up his headquarters on his temple grounds so he could better oversee the slaughter of his fellow monks atop the mount.

Sitting well away from Ōsu's highways, the temple grounds breathed the same quietude that must have instilled a sense of calm in all those who entered them since the temple's foundation during the middle of the 9th century. A hushed silence lay over the forty-odd structures that now make up the temple complex. Except for a few janitors who were getting ready for the chores of the day, not a soul could be seen along the wide unpaved avenue that connects the Gon-*dō* to the Kannon-*dō* atop a raised platform at the south end of the complex.

The location scouts of Japan's film industry had clearly also discovered the temple and its beautiful setting. All along the avenue stood notices of the films for which scenes had been shot on location. Though the posters were already jaded, the films they advertised were not that old. One of them was *Rurō ni Kenshin*, the story of a *rorō*, a 'wandering samurai' by the name of Kenshin (Sword Spirit) set in early Meiji Japan. It was a 2012 film adaptation of *Rorō ni Kenshin: Swordsman Romantic Story*, a popular *manga* series by Nobuhiro Watsuki, which ran into twenty-eight volumes and sold more than seventy million copies worldwide. Crammed with spine-defying live-action scenes, these films are a natural continuation of the *chambara eiga*, a genre that came into its own during Japan's post-war years. Invariably centered around a lone sword-yielding hero, they were the rough equivalent to the Errol Flynn-type swashbuckling movies of the Golden Age of Hollywood.

Not all the films advertised along the temple's avenue were about male prowess with the sword. Other films, more in keeping with the temple's tranquil setting, were also on display. *Bushi no Kondate*, for instance. Know by the English title *A Tale of Samurai Cooking*, this film from 2013 tells the story of a highly talented female cook who marries into a family of renowned hereditary cooks. To her horror she soon discovers that, though pretty good at wielding his two swords, her husband has failed to inherit his father's talent of handling

144

a kitchen knife: the food from his hands is simply awful. It so happens that the food he prepares is not served to any old lord but to Lord Maeda Shigehiro, a stickler for high-end cuisine. And so the resourceful heroine decides to save her husband's honor by initiating him into the secrets of good cooking and thereby salvage the clan's reputation. In this, she is not at all helped by her husband, who was forced to pursue his father's profession after his older brother suddenly

*View of Lake Biwa from the terrace of the Kannon-*dō

passed away and prefers to dabble in highly conspiratorial clan politics. Apart from taking a critical look at Japan's traditional gender roles, the movie presents an interesting window into the cooking traditions and eating habits of Edo period Japanese, albeit of course the eating habits of those among the higher echelons of feudal society.

By the time I had reviewed all the films that had been shot at the Mii Temple, I had reached the Golden Hall. There I was drawn by a mysterious gurgling sound, which turned out to come from a well behind the hall, just left of the Kumano Gongen Shrine. The well, called the Amaya no I, was enclosed in a small latticed building. I put my face close up to the lattices, and though I could see a small puddle among some rocks, I could not tell if the gurgling was caused by spring water welling up from the depths of the earth or from one of those giant Japanese toads who had made the place its dwelling, in which case I preferred not to know.

The view from the temple must have been stunning in Kaempfer's time. From the elevated terrace in front of the temple's Kannon-*dō*, it still was. Across Lake Biwa, toward the northeast, I could clearly make out the peaks of the Ibuki Sanchi, the mountain range that separates east from west Japan, its only passage the Imasu Pass, near the old battlegrounds of Sekigahara.

At the end of the flight of stairs down from the terrace stood a small ticket booth. As I passed it, I was startled by the sound of a small window at its front sliding open with a bang. Through it peeked an elderly lady who, still out of breath, had clearly just installed herself. She smiled apologetically as she explained, 'Sorry, but I'm afraid you still have to pay the entrance fee.'

Minakuchi

Okamura-*san*, another kindly lady at the counter of the small museum within the former inner citadel of what once was Minakuchi Castle, seemed happy to have a visitor. I had almost skipped the castle as the beautiful old wooden bridge at its entrance had been blocked, and the castle seemed quite abandoned.

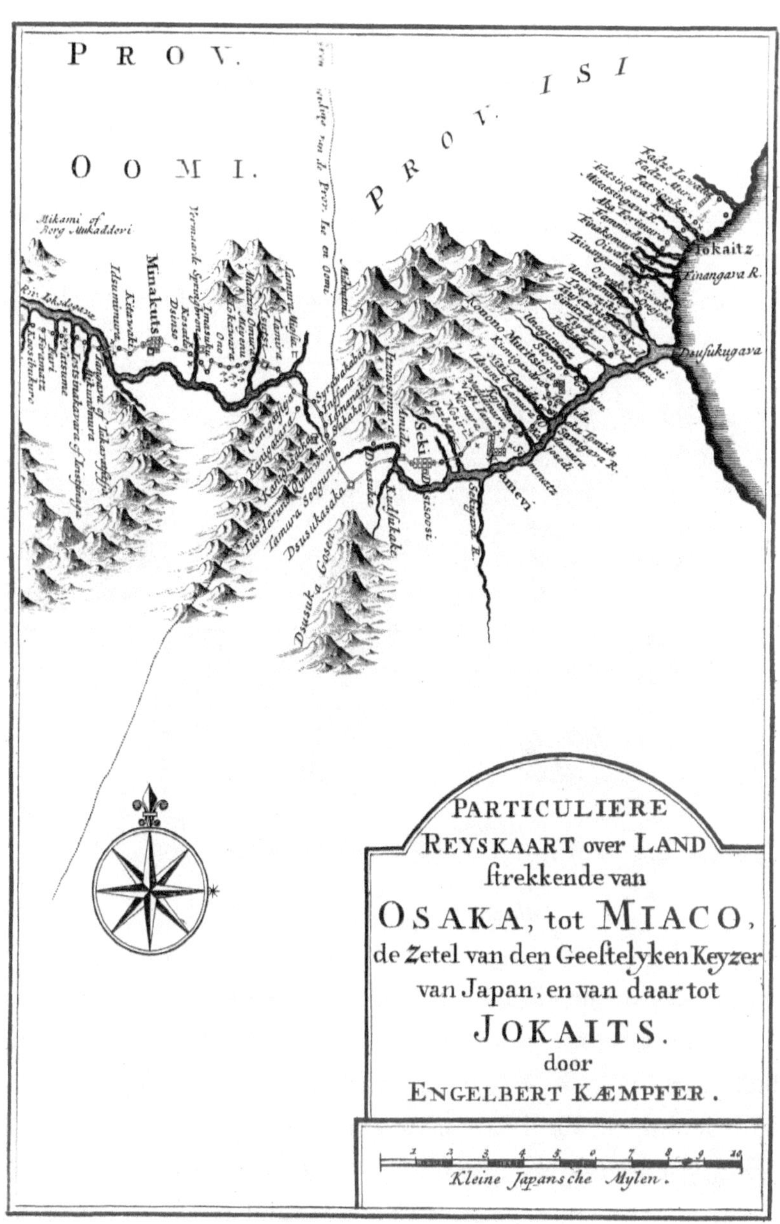

From Minakuchi to Yokkaichi

'Yes,' she said mournfully, 'the bridge is in very bad repair and there is no money to restore it.' She led me to a screen in a corner of the room and we both watched an eight-minute video about the castle's history.

Minakuchi had started out as just one of the Tōkaidō's fifty-three post towns. That all changed in the years leading up to 1638, when *Shōgun* Tokugawa Iemitsu planned to spend the night at Minakuchi

Minakuchi Castle's poorly bridge

on his way to the capital Kyoto. A huge workforce of carpenters under the supervision of Kobori Masakazu (1579–1647) set out to build a vast multi-roomed palace to accommodate the *shōgun* and his large retinue. It was the same kind of opulent palace I had visited a few days earlier on the grounds of Nijō Castle's second bailey. Yet it was only used once. Even after the castle and its palace became the official seat of *Daimyō* Katō Akitomo (1621–84), he refrained from

148

taking up residence at his palace in deference to the Tokugawa. Finally, during the early 18th century, the palace was dismantled, having stood empty for close to a century.

Suzuka Pass

The high grass along the road toward the Suzaka Pass had just been cut and despite the exhaust fumes of the passing trucks, it smelt like the interior of a Japanese house with fresh *tatami* mats. There was even the sound of a small mountain stream, though it was pouring down a concrete duct.

Some six hundred feet below the top of the pass, the tarmac road ended and went over into a sandy path that disappeared into a dense wood. To take away my last doubts, there was a stone pillar engraved with the characters 'Tōkaidō,' Another pillar read, 'From here to Miyako 17 *ri*' and 'From here to Edo 190 *ri*.' A *ri* was the feudal equivalent of roughly 2.4 miles. I still had some way to go.

Just into the quiet woods a small *jizō*, its features all but withered away, guarded over those who passed. I placed a few coins in the small saucer at its foot and went my way.

After the Hiyamizu Pass, it was the second pass since my departure from Nagasaki. I braced myself for another stiff climb but it was all over before I knew it. Following a faint climb and a short descent, I came out onto a clearing, its view blocked by the elevated Tōkaidō Expressway.

From there onwards it was all downhill to the old post town of Seki. But not scenic-wise. Once I had passed under the expressway, the path went over into the kind of paved surface I had found along sections of the Nakasendō and Nagasaki Kaidō. Like Kaepmpfer and those who went after him, I descended down steep slopes at sharp angles, passing under fir trees that were thin but at least a hundred feet tall:

> The descent of this mountain is not unlike that of a winding staircase, some broad stone steps hewn out of the border of

Entrance to the Suzaka Pass

> a deep precipice, leading down to another neighboring mountain, which is very remarkable for being a sort of a weather glass to the pilots of this country, who by its top being clear, or covered with clouds, and some other signs, know how the weather is likely to prove, and consequently whether or not it be safe for them to venture out to sea, on their voyages.

Lower down, where the path began to follow a mountain brook, stood a small shrine atop a bulwark of large stones that had been stacked with the same technique used in castle walls. A stone pillar declared it to be the Katayama Shrine. Was it this shrine that Kaempfer described during his descent?

> We were full a quarter of an hour coming down the mountain. At the foot, we took notice of another chapel, before which stood a gilt lion. Some priests presented here to travelers a relic to kiss, and by way of reward took from them a farthing a piece.

No gilt lion guarded the entrance, but high up, atop a long flight of stairs, still sat a small shrine. Guarding the southern entrance to the pass, the shrine has a long history that goes back to the early Heian period. Legend has it that the pass—an important traffic artery between the old provinces of Ise and Ōmi—was made unsafe by a 'celestial maiden' by the name of Suzaka Gozen. Word of her predations reached the ear of Sakanoue no Tamuramaro (758–811), captain of the Right Division of Inner Palace Guards. He decided to punish her, but having hunted her down, he fell under her spell and married her. Ever since, her spirit has been worshipped at the shrine, not as a highway robber but as a guardian deity who watches over all who cross the pass.

Looking back from the village of Sakashita or 'At the Foot of the Slope,' the pass I had just traversed still seemed formidable, for the mountains towered high in the distance. The village, too, had lost little of the charm it must have had for the Dutch travelers two centuries earlier.

Shrine at the foot of the Suzaka Pass

The next hamlet, Naranoki, nestled at the foot of Mt. Fudesute, was equally charming. I had to look up the mountain's name afterward, for an elderly woman, a black and white cat curling at her feet, who said she had lived there all her life, wasn't able to enlighten me. Then, reading back Siebold's account, I found he held the answer:

> We passed a mountain by the name of Fudesute-*yama*, which means, 'throw-away-one's-brush mountain.' The name has its origin in a legend that relates how the famous painter Kano, when trying to paint the mountain, threw away his brush as the mountain kept changing its shape while he was painting.

After Naranoki it was all over, as the old Tōkaidō Highway route merged with the new Tōkaidō Expressway. But I could still enjoy the densely wooded and steep mountains that attended my descent into Seki, to marvel at their undiminished beauty as Kanō Motonobu (1476–1569) had done more than half a millennium before me.

Seki

Apart from (Kaempfer) mentioning that Seki consisted of roughly a hundred houses whose inhabitants made a living making hats, shoes, and matches out of split reeds, none of our Mission's chroniclers dwell at length on the post town. And why should they? It was just another post town in a very long string of post towns along their one-thousand-mile-long route. Today, Seki is one of the few, arguably the only post town along the Tōkaidō that has been preserved. Consequently, those who dwell in Seki no longer need to split reeds but can make a good living from the tourism it attracts.

Passing through Seki Kaempfer also described a large number of pilgrims:

Among the pilgrims we met this day, there was a woman well dressed in silk, and strongly painted, leading a blind old man

Seki, almost unchanged since the Edo period

and begging before him, which we thought a very extraordinary sight. We also met several young *bikuni*, a sort of begging nuns (of which I have already given some account in the 5th chapter of this book) who accost travelers for their charity, singing some songs to divert them, though upon a strange wild sort of a tune. They will stay with them for a small matter as long as they desire it. Most of them are daughters of the *yamabushi*, or mountain priests, and consecrated as sisters of this holy begging order, by having their heads shaved. They go neatly and well clad, wearing a black silk hood upon their shaved heads, and a light hat over it to defend their faces from the heat of the sun. Their behavior is to all appearance modest and free, neither too bold and loose, nor too dejected and mean. As to their persons, they are as great beauties as one shall see in this country. In short, the whole scene is more like a comedy, than the begging of indigent and poor people. It is true indeed, their fathers could not send out, upon the begging errand, persons more fit for it, since they know not only how to come at traveller's purses, but have charms and beauties enough to oblige them to farther good services. For distinction's sake, from other begging nuns, they are called Kumano *bikuni*, because they go always two and two, and have their stations assigned them only upon the roads hereabouts. They are obliged to bring so much a year, of what they get by begging, to the temple at Ise, by way of a tribute.

It is not surprising that Kaempfer should have encountered so many pilgrims at Seki. The town formed the crossroads of the Tōkaidō and the Ise Sangū Kaidō, the old high road to the Grand Shrine of Ise. Already then, a cult had evolved around the shrine, and pilgrims from all over the country would take our time to visit the shrine at least once in their lifetime. One of the reasons it became so popular was that most people weren't allowed to cross the border into other domains without being in possession of strictly regulated permits. Only when they went on a pilgrimage were these restrictions lifted, so that for many (even farmers, who weren't allowed to travel at all) it was a safe way to have a vacation and see how green the grass was on the other side. This form of travel grew exponentially with the abolishment of the old barriers and the growing safety of travel during the Edo period. Where the number of pilgrims during the first years of the Edo period hovered around twenty to thirty thousand a year, by the middle of the same period, it had grown tenfold. In certain years, the number of pilgrims on the road to Ise reached staggering proportions. These were the so-called *o-kagetoshi* or 'thank you years.' In those years pilgrims came to celebrate the shrine's rebuilding, for tradition dictated that a shrine be dismantled and freshly rebuilt every twenty years. It is believed, for instance, that in the *o-kagetoshi*-year of 1705 alone, the shrine was visited by some three million pilgrims—more than a tenth of Japan's total population at the time.

Kameyama

After three-quarters of an hour's riding, we came to the town of Kameyama, which lies on a rising ground, or the flat top of an eminence. It is a pretty large town, taken in with a wall, as far as I could see, and likewise defended with strong gates and guards. On the south-side of the town stands the castle, tolerably well fortified with ditches, walls, and round bastions. We were riding near an hour before we got to the third guard, and to the end of the suburbs, the streets running very irregularly, because of the unevenness of the ground, on which the town stands.

Unlike Kaempfer's and most other Missions, which usually took lunch at Kameyama and traveled on to spend the night at Yokkaichi, I decided to stay the night. To escape the gloom of the rundown business hotel I was staying at, I went out to have something to eat. I ended up in a modern *kaiten sushi* restaurant, where the *sushi* is delivered to your seat on a small conveyor belt. This one was more than modern. Stepping inside, I was directed to a console with a

Kameyama Caste's Tamon Turret

touchscreen into which I had to punch whether I wanted to eat in or out (in), with how many I was (one), and whether I wanted to eat in a booth or at the counter (the latter). It disgorged a ticket with a QR code and a number that was eventually called out by a robotic voice while the number was displayed on an overhead screen. Having scanned my QR code at the console, I received another ticket, this time with my number at the counter.

Unlike the *kaiten sushi* I was used to from my days in Tokyo, some thirty years ago, there were no saucers with *sushi* on a circular conveyor belt. Nor were there any *sushi* chefs behind the counter welcoming new customers with a hearty '*Irasshai!*' Instead, a straight conveyor belt ran into and through a wall, behind which I presumed the *sushi* chefs—or were it *sushi* robots?—were frantically at work to meet the orders (there were three such belts in a row). At yet another display at my seat I could place my orders, each of which was greeted with a robotic but surprisingly natural-sounding, '*Go-chūmon, arigatō gozaimashita!*' thanking me for my order. After a few moments, the conveyor belt began to spin, and a saucer with my *sushi* appeared through the wall, rapidly moving toward me, then slowing down and halting exactly in front of my seat.

The next morning, I visited the Kameyama Museum of History. It, too, was located on the grounds of the local castle. The area's history went back for thousands of years—recently unearthed stone arrow tips and urn-like coffins point to the early Jōmon period (4000–400 BC). Judging by the coffins, its dwellers were almost pigmy-like. A display of an excavated burial mound found at nearby Idagawa illustrated how, by the Kofun period (300–538), dignitaries were buried in flat coffins chiselled out of stone, not unlike those recently unearthed at the Yoshinogari Historic Park halfway between Saga and Kurume. Delicate necklaces, gold-plated earrings, and finely decorated shards of pottery reveal that their civilization had reached a remarkable level of refinement. It was concentrated along a wedge of fertile land between the Suzuka and Anraku rivers. And it was there that, some nine hundred years ago, a small town was formed. The first to mention the name Kameyama was the Heian court official Watarai Tomoatsu when he wrote a report to his superiors at the imperial court in Kyoto.

Kameyama really came into its own during the Edo period when, as the capital of the Ise Kameyama domain, it grew into a flourishing castle town. A large maquette in the museum's main exhibition hall gave a good impression of its scale and how its main vectors of expansion were determined by the route the Tōkaidō took along Kameyama Castle. It also proved that Kaempfer must have been disoriented when he claimed the castle lay south of the town; the opposite was true.

Kuwana

Kuwana is a very large city and the first in the Province of Owari. It lies on a large and spacious harbor, or rather gulf of Ise Bay, which runs a good way up into the country. It consists of three different parts, as so many different towns. We were full three quarters of an hour before we came to our inn, which was at the extremity of the third. The first part of the city is taken in with a high wall and ditches, as is also the third. The gates are strong and well guarded. The second, or middle part, has no walls, but is entirely surrounded with water, the country being flat and full of rivers.

On the south-side of the third part stands the castle and residence of Matsudaira Sadashige, built in the water. Its walls are very high, with loopholes broke through and neatly covered with a roof. Blockhouses are built on them, at small distances. This castle takes in a large square spot of ground. The eastside only is a little roundish. A deep and large ditch divides it from the city, over which, for communication's sake are laid two bridges. Three sides of it are washed by the sea. In the middle of the castle there is a square white tower rising aloft several stories high, with several roofs according to the country's fashion, which adds very much to the beauty of the place. This castle was built by *Shōgun* Tokugawa Ietsuna, uncle of the now reigning monarch, who having a natural aversion to the female sex, but more particularly to the empress his spouse, ordered, that she, together with the ladies of her court, and his the *shōgun*'s own nurse, should spend therein the remainder of their lives.

Today, the three townships described by Kaempfer have merged into a faceless city with no charm. I had thought Ōmura was a dump but compared to Kuwana it was heaven. It seemed those who lived around the city agreed, for I hadn't seen so many bust shops and restaurants on my whole trip thus far, their shutters closed never to open again. Such streets are known in Japan as *shattaa-dōri* or, 'shutter streets.'

Fully in tune with the rest of Kuwana, all that was left of its impressive seaside castle was a vague impression of its former outline imprinted on the layout of Kyūka Park. None of its manyfold buildings remained. The only structure that looked like it might have belonged to the castle was a recreation of the stronghold's Banryū-*yagura*. A concrete structure resembling a turret, it actually serves as a control station for the sluices at the mouth of the castle's northern moat, which still is the home of Kuwana's modest fishing fleet.

I was hungry and bought myself a *bentō* at a local supermarket. I ate it on the windy steps toward the concrete embankment of the Ibi River. Due east, across a stretch of reclaimed land at the head of

Ise Bay, I could make out the high-rise buildings of Nagoya's city center. Toward the north, following the river upstream, I could see the southern reaches of the Ifuku Mountain range plummeting into the river delta. Beyond them, on the plains of Sekigahara, Ieyasu had crossed his first Rubicon.

Nearby, a huge wooden *torii* marked the Shichiri no Watashi, the place from where travelers bound for Edo would embark in small

The Shichiri no Watashi

boats to be ferried across the foot of the bay toward Miya, from where they would continue their journey over land along the Tōkaidō. *Shichiri* means 'seven *ri*,' the distance over water between the ports of Kuwana and Miya. There was also a Sanri no Watashi, or 'Three *Ri* Ferry,' which would merely put you across the Ibi and Kiso rivers and land you at the Saya post town on the east bank of the Kiso River. But most of the time, the wide river delta was considered too treacherous. There were no bridges, and heavy downpours during typhoons would turn the area into a floodplain impassable for weeks.

I was reminded of just how much destruction the seasonal typhoons can wreak by a nearby monument commemorating the victims of typhoon Vera. Reaching wind speeds of up to 90 m/s, it raged over the Ise Bay during the last days of September 1959. In its wake, it left a trail of destruction only surpassed in the last year of the war of just

The Nagara Estuary Barrier

fourteen years earlier. It swept away more than thirty thousand homes, damaged thrice the number, killed more than five thousand, and wounded close to forty thousand. Some thirty prefectures were affected but the hardest hit were Aichi and Mie. Much of the damage wrought came in its wake, caused by the staggering amount of rain it unleashed. In the village of Kawagami, the daily precipitation for the 26th alone reached 650 mm—more than half a meter! This, combined with

162

breached sea barriers around the bay, caused countless of the still-standing houses in the low-lying delta to be flooded. With the limited post-war resources, it took more than half a year to drain the flooded area. By then, the affected houses had become uninhabitable.

It was purportedly to protect the river delta from future flooding that, the following year, the Japanese Ministry of Construction launched a plan to build a barrier in the estuary of the Nagara River. To their surprise, they were vehemently opposed by the locals, who organized themselves into the Society Against the Nagara Estuary Dam. They were a motley crew, consisting of fishermen, canoeists, nature lovers, and people generally opposed to turning all of Japan's rivers into concrete water ducts. This is not an exaggeration; by the time they launched their campaign's final push in 1998, after a struggle of almost four decades, the Nagara River was the one remaining natural major river on the main island of Honshū.

The activists argued that, far from protecting the locals from flooding, the barrier actually posed an additional threat in that water levels behind the barrier would be artificially kept at 1.3 m above sea level, and this while the towns on both sides of the barrier were below. It would also prevent migrating fish like trout from making their passage up and down the river.

The campaign gained real traction in the run-up of the Rio Earth Summit of 1992, the campaign quickly gained traction. Membership climbed to 16,000 and after much political lobbying, they managed to persuade half the Diet members to sign a petition against the dam's construction. They were also backed by the director general of Japan's Environment Agency, who conceded that the barrier 'might increase the danger of flooding and do harm to the ecology of the river.'

It was to no avail. The ironclad pact between politicians and the construction companies that finance their costly campaigns ensured the project went ahead nonetheless. And so, from my vantage point of the ferro-cement Banryū Turret, I could admire the row of giant doors that now form the Nagara Estuary Barrier.

Miya

Just how tricky the Shichiri no Watashi could be is revealed by Kaempfer's description of his Mission crossing the Saya River:

> Vast quantities of wood are floated down this river, out of the province of Owari, and several other places. The harbor is very shallow, and full of muddy banks, which stand up in low water four or six foot. This shallowness obliged us to leave the four large boats we had hired for our passage, about an hour before we came to Miya, and to make use of smaller ones, for us and our baggage, as far as that city. These small boats were drawn, or rather pulled, over the muddy banks by the help of poles of bamboo, two men being appointed for each boat, one before, and another behind. This singular kind of navigation, though it seemed to us strangers, that were not used to it, very ridiculous and odd, went on very well, the upper surface of the mud being very soft and smooth, the ground hard and the boats small, containing not above seven or eight persons, and still less, if laden with other goods. Accordingly we came to Miya betimes, about two hours before sunset.

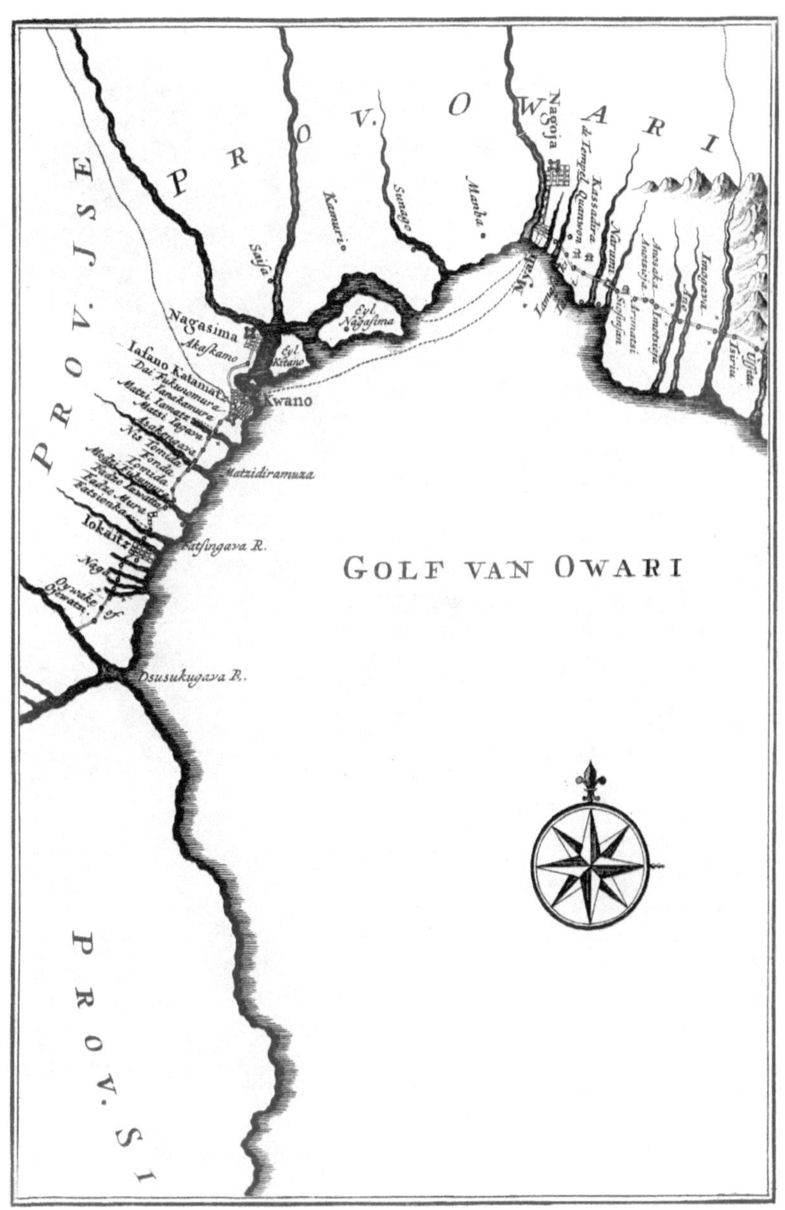

Yokkaichi to Nagoya

Miya's old lighthouse

The ferry landing at Miya is still marked by the port's old lighthouse. It no longer casts its beam over the Bay of Ise, but now has to make do with a wide canal through a two-mile stretch of reclaimed land. In the old days, Miya was one of the more interesting spots among the Tōkaidō's fifty-three stations, as the Shichiri no Watashi was the only section that was done over open water. It was immortalized in many contemporary wood prints, among others by Utagawa Hiroshige.

On Kaempfer, the hamlet of Miya made little impression:

> Miya has no walls: There is only a sorry ditch both going in and coming out of the town. It is very populous and large, though not quite so large as Kuwana, consisting only of about two thousand houses. On the right is a square palace built in the form of a castle, where the *shōgun* lodges on his journey to Kyoto, as do also some of the greatest princes of the empire in their journeys to and from court. The streets run across each other, with as much regularity as the disposition of the ground would admit of.

Kaempfer's 'sorry ditch' was the Hori Canal, a prestigious feat of civil engineering under the supervision of Fukushima Masanori. Dug in 1610 by a vast army of forced laborers, the canal was used to transport the huge stones and beams used in the expansion of Nagoya Castle, then the residence of Ieyasu's ninth son Tokugawa Yoshinao (1601–50).

Miya, and its 'sorry ditch,' then, were the nautical gateway to the city of Nagoya, though of course there was also an overland thoroughfare:

A long street, or row of houses, runs for near two miles from Miya, and terminates at Nagoya, the residence of the lord of this province, who is a prince of the Tokugawa line. The castle, wherein he resides, is reckoned the third in the empire for strength and extent. It is with the utmost magnificence this prince makes his journey to court. Only his vanguards consists of upwards of 2000 men, with led-horses, halberds, pikes, bows, arrows and other arms, baskets, trunks, and numberless other things, some for use, some for state, all with his coat of arms upon them. When the Dutch meet him upon the road, the whole retinue must alight from their horses, our resident come out of his *norimono*, and all in silent humble posture, out of respect for the Tokugawa, stay till he has been carried by.

The thoroughfare from Saya to Nagoya formed the first stretch of the Saya Kaidō, the high road skirting the river estuaries at the head of Ise Bay to terminate at the Saya post town on the east bank of the Kiso River. The Tōkaidō itself picked up its route from Miya to continue southeastward toward Ieayasu's hometown of Okazaki. This meant that the Missions bypassed the city of Nagoya. The closest they came was the famous Atsuta Shrine, just a stone's throw from Miya and, even in Siebold's time, situated on the city's outskirts:

Going through Miya we passed by a small Shintō shrine, which had been rebuilt four years ago, and remarkably is called Atsuta, or the Temple of the Three Scimitars. Two red gates, such as are usually to be seen before temples, stand at its entrance. Three miraculous scimitars, which had been used in the ancient times of that race of demigods, who inhabited this country,

168

and carried on cruel wars against each other, are preserved in this temple as sacred relics. They were kept formerly in the temple at Ise, from whence about the time, above mentioned, they were removed hither. Five Shintō priests attended at this temple, clad in white ecclesiastical gowns, with black lacquered caps, such as are worn at the court of the *dairi*, or ecclesiastical hereditary emperor. Two of the lowest rank stood on the floor

Nagoya's Atsuta Shrine

of the temple, two others of a higher rank sate behind them somewhat raised, and the fifth sate about the middle of the temple, placed higher than all the rest.

Needless to say, the Atsuta Shrine has meanwhile been swallowed up by Nagoya's suburbs. But passing under the huge *torii* and walking up the long avenue toward the shrine's *honden* in the shade of pines one can still share in the delight millions of pilgrims must have felt on visiting the shrine since it was founded during the middle of the 7th century. Only second to the Ise Jingū, it has a rich history and was the place from where Oda Nobunaga, having made his offerings, once set out to claim his first victory in his quest to rule the realm. Though the *honden* itself is still of modest proportions, the shrine has since grown into a large complex that can host wedding ceremonies and other auspicious events in a lavish way. I happen to know because I once attended one. But that is a different story.

Okazaki

Okazaki is a very large town, and the residence of the lord of this province. We dined here, having travelled this morning seven miles. Okazaki reckons about 1500 houses, most of which are well built. It is enclosed with a neat hedge, or palisade of bamboo, and in some places with a wall. The castle lies on the south-end of the town on a hill, and is enclosed with ditches, and a white wall raised on a low rampart. The wall is defended with strong guardhouses built of stone at different distances. Towards the hill, where it is most liable to an attack, it is defended with a triple strong wall. The high tower in the middle of the castle, the usual mark of princely residences, shows itself on the southwest-side to admiration.

The suburbs I found to consist of about 200 houses. A large river, which has its name from the city, runs across it. This river, though pretty broad and not wanting water, is yet not navigable, being very shallow. It arises in the neighboring

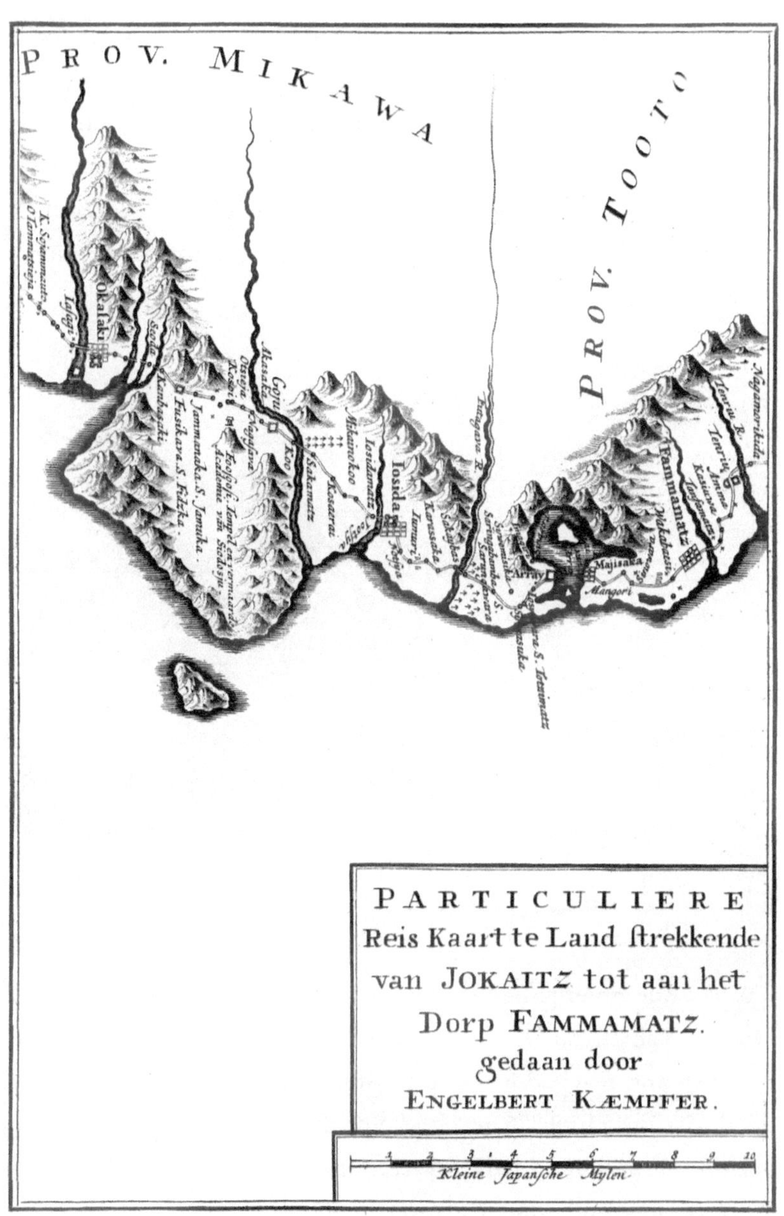

Okazaki to Hamamatsu

mountains to the northwest, from whence it continues its course with great rapidity, till it loses itself into the sea. A strong and magnificent wooden bridge is laid over it, which the Japanese say is 158 *ken*, or fathoms long, but my servant measuring it, found it to be of 350 paces in length. From our entering the suburbs, we were half a mile going to our inn, which was a very magnificent one.

The Yahagi Bridge as depicted by Utagawa Hiroshige

When Kaempfer passed through Okazaki, its castle was the seat of Mizuno Tadamitsu (1663–99). The Mizuno clan's ties to Okazaki ran deep and reached far back in time. Tadamitsu was already the third Mizuno chieftain in charge of the domain. And way back, during the middle of the 16th century, the daughter of his great-great-great-grandfather Tadamasa, a young woman by the name of Odai no Kata (1528-1602), had given birth at his castle to a child by

172

the name of Takechiyo. Coming of age at fourteen, Takechiyo became known as Matsudaira Motoyasu. The young warrior suffered the first of his few defeats at nearby Okehazama, fighting against the brilliant warlord Oda Nobunaga. He survived by the skin of his teeth, making it back to his ancestral home of Okazaki Castle. From there he began to plot his ascent, forging alliances with powerful warlords, first with Oda Nobunaga, then with Takeda Shigen, and

Today's Yahagi Bridge

finally with Toyotomi Hideyoshi. By then, he had assumed the name by which he would be known to posterity: Tokugawa Ieyasu, founder of the Tokugawa, a dynasty that was to rule Japan for two and a half centuries.

Making my way from the castle to the Yahagi no Hashi, the famed bridge Kaempfer describes, it was easy to tell that Okazaki was proud of its Tokugawa credentials. Every shrine, temple, gate, statue—even a stone with a special shape—I passed claimed some connection to the great man and his time at Okazaki.

The Yahagi no Hashi actually started out as a plain mud dam across the eponymous river. It was swept away by floods so often that, halfway through the 17th century, it was replaced by a wooden bridge. There were only few such structures during the Edo period—the Nihonbashi Bridge in Edo, the Seta Bridge near Kyoto, and the Kintai Bridge at Iwakuni being the most prominent—but at 378 m the Yahagi no Hashi was the longest and a marvel for all who crossed it. Of course the wooden bridge Kaempfer, Siebold, and Fischer admired no longer exists. It was replaced by a cast iron bridge on cast iron girders in 1913. When the new bridge, which stood slightly farther upstream, collapsed in the 1945 Mikawa Earthquake, it was replaced by a steel bridge on concrete pylons. It stood until 2006 when, due to wear and tear, it was no longer deemed safe and replaced by the present one. Cast out of concrete and steel and curved like a Japanese sword, the bridge refuses the kind of pretense upheld by the Seta Bridge but boldly claims its modern pedigree.

Yoshida

Halfway between Okazaki and Toyohashi—or what was still known as Yoshida during the Edo period—I was entering the countryside again. The hills that had remained in the far distance toward the northeast began to draw nearer and the villages had a rural feel again. I passed a group of young men, *tenugui* towels wrapped around their heads, who were pushing a portable shrine on wheels into a large shed.

At one stretch, the road was flanked on both sides by pine trees. For those who mightn't have realized, a signpost reminded them it was something exceptional. It was the Goyu Pine Colonnade. Cars and motorbikes kept whizzing past, even though the National Highway Route 1 was just a few trailer lengths away. The stretch of trees was no more than half a mile, yet it was still enough to instill a sense of calm as I dodged the oncoming cars.

The Goyu Pine (Car) Colonnade

How much more pleasant it was to walk among the greenery, the fragrance of pine resin in one's nostrils. And how much cooler too. It was a reasonably hot day, but in the shade of the pines, it was at least five degrees less. Why oh why, I wondered, did one have to travel half the length of Japan to experience such simple joys? Why couldn't they for once divert the traffic? And what on earth is so difficult about planting a few trees? It wasn't that these trees had been planted by the present powers that be; they were a relic of the *bakufu*'s deliberate policy of lining Japan's high roads with pine trees to provide shade and comfort to all who had to be on the road.

Farther along, in a bend of the Otowa River, a child was amusing itself by throwing stones in the rushing water. It still knew where the fun was.

Another site of historic interest in Toyohashi is Yoshida Castle. It still carries the name by which the city too used to be known, until the latter was changed to Toyohashi during the early Meiji period. In Kaempfer's day, it was a formidable stronghold:

> The castle stands on the northeast side of the town, and is a square building, as usual. Three sides of it are enclosed with walls and ditches, on the fourth it is defended by a river, which runs by it. The walls are high, white and neat, otherwise without guardhouses, or any other defense, the castle having been built only to receive and lodge the princes of the empire in their journies to and from court. The lord of this castle had ordered a file of twenty *bugyō*, or soldiers of the first rank, to receive us under arms, in order to honor our passage. There is a great deal of smith's work made and sold here. I took notice that the country people had brought great quantities of wood, leaves, hay, peas, and other produce of the country to market, perhaps because it was a market day at the place.

In the tiny exhibition within the ferro-cement reconstruction of the castle's keep, there were just a few items on display: an old and tattered harness, and two scale models, one of its inner citadel, and one of the castle's full layout done in white plaster so that it looked

176

like a winter castle-scape. The rest of the exhibition consisted of old maps and illustrations with explanatory texts: of the nearby Yoshida Bridge, of the Maeshiba Lighthouse at the mouth of the Toyo River, and of the post station where the Mission's members spent the night before they traveled on to Arai. To me, the most interesting item was an 1883 photograph of a get-together of former retainers of the Yoshida domain, already all of them without topknots. On their faces,

Yoshida Castle

they wore a somewhat jaded expression, though I could not make out whether they yearned for the old days or for the benefits of a modern and Westernized Japan.

Toyohashi's other main historic site is Futugawa-*juku*. In Kaempfer's time, Futagawa was the next post town along the Tōkaidō from Yoshida and the thirty-third when counting from Edo. A small section of the former post town is carefully preserved at Toyohashi's Futagawa Township, just five miles east along the Tōkaidō from the castle.

The post town's history is told at the Futagawa-*juku Honjin* Museum. The *honjin* was a post town's main inn, the place where *daimyō* and other high officials spent the night before they moved on to the next post town. The word *honjin* actually means 'field headquarters,' the place where a feudal chieftain set up camp when

*The Futugawa-*juku Honjin *Museum*

out campaigning and from which he rode into battle. How that term also came to be applied to these official inns is not exactly clear. Its first usage as such can be traced back to 1634, when, en route to the capital, *Shōgun* Tokugawa Iemitsu appointed all landlords of the inns at which he intended to stay to the post of *honjin-yaku*, or 'camp duty.' It seems that, with the introduction of the *sankin kōtai* system just a year later, the term *honjin* stuck.

178

The museum, which is housed in the actual *honjin*, did a good job of conveying the luxury in which *daimyō* and their entourage (as well as the Mission's senior members) used to travel. A wide entrance draped with curtains emblazoned with the crest of the Mizuno clan led on to a wide *genkan* and spacious rooms that impress the visitor with their sober but refined choice of materials. The main guest room, at which a *daimyō* could receive guests

*Futagawa-*juku *as depicted by Utagawa Hiroshige*

during his stay at the inn, had a wide *tokonoma* or 'alcove' in which a seasonal scroll and matching *ikebana* provided the topic for a pleasant conversation. Nearby, just down a corridor encircling a rectangular inner garden, was the *o-furo*, a bathhouse in which a large *hinoki* bathtub took center stage.

For those lower down the scale of feudal society there were the *hatago*, one of which is preserved right next to the Futagawa *Honjin*.

Hatago means 'traveling basket,' a term used for the baskets in which travelers kept the feed for their horses. With time, travelers also began to refer to their own food baskets as *hatago*, which in turn led innkeepers to humbly refer to their establishment with the same term. Futagawa had some thirty such *hatago*. Upon entering the *hatago*, I was immediately struck by the more cramped space, and though it still boasted a bathroom, it was barely large enough to fit the half-sized tub. The fare served at these lesser inns wasn't that bad, really. In his diary titled *Sendai gekō nikki* (*Going Down to Sendai*), the Osaka merchant Masuya Heiemon (1764–1836) describes how he spends the nights at a *hatago* in the post town of Tarui along the Nakasendō. The menu for that evening reads 'Grey mullet, served with dried horse radish and bamboo shoots.' For breakfast, he and his fellow travelers are served an assortment of 'Japanese amberjack, *shiitake* mushrooms, butterbur, steamed buns, bracken, and *tōfu*.' It might not appeal to the average Western hotel guest but it certainly sounds a lot healthier than the high-cholesterol fare of 'Wiener sausage, fried bacon, and omelet' on offer at your run-of-the-mill Japanese business hotel. Those who want to experience the real thing still can; for even today, a number of *hatago*, roughly a dozen throughout the country, still serve traditional menus, and a few will even put you up for the night, though no longer in Futagawa.

Arai

The stretch from Toyohashi to Arai was long, hot, and uneventful. I knew I had to prepare myself for much of the same over the coming days as I had walked this stretch of the Tōkaidō before. Traveling in the opposite direction, I had grown so bored that, just to get away from it all, I had jumped on a bus down the Atsui Peninsula and taken the ferry across the bay to Ise. This time, I was determined to slog it out, but I knew it would take grit and determination.

Arai, I remembered, formed a blip in the drabness that lay ahead, and I was determined to make the most of it. It is the place where two headlands meet to embrace the natural lagoon of Lake Hanama. The Tōkaidō followed both headlands to their tips, at which point travelers had to take a ferry to cross the narrow strait at the head of the lagoon. It was a picturesque place, immortalized in woodblock prints by Utagawa Hiroshige and others. Especially its blindingly bone-white sands, sands that stretched all the way from Cape Irago on the Atsui Peninsula to Cape Omaesaki, cast a spell on those who walked them, among them Siebold:

> A strong surf, just as the tide was coming in again, struck a
> beech covered with fine sand, and as the waves heaved away,
> a glimmering film cast the mirror-like surface in a golden sheen.

The sands at Arai must have been stunning indeed, so much so that Siebold—a man otherwise so attuned to the historicity of a place— forgot to mention Arai's important role as a barrier.

The history of the Arai-*sekisho*, or the 'Arai Barrier Office,' was told in the nearby Sekisho History Museum. The *bakufu*'s one-time office is still there and, changing into slippers, one can walk its corridors to peek into its Edo-period rooms. An exhibition in a two-story annex explained how the barrier was established almost immediately after Ieyasu had attained his victory at Sekigahara and was in control of most of the realm. It was effectively a border control; all who passed it had to submit passports specifying the purpose of their journey. The only difference was that such barriers were not necessarily placed at borders between provinces but at strategic positions along Japan's major highways. By the middle of the Edo period, there were some fifty-three such barriers. Nineteen of them were considered important, but the one at Kiso Fukushima along

The Arai Sekisho History Museum

the Nakasendō, and the ones at Hakone and Arai along the Tōkaidō were considered crucial.

It all, of course, had to do with safeguarding the Tokugawa seat of government in Edo. Unlike in earlier times, no taxes were levied. Nor did one need a special permit if one were carrying firearms, just a decent explanation, as long as one was traveling away from Edo. Things were quite different if one was traveling up to Edo (they called it 'traveling down,' since Kyoto was still the capital). In that case, one not only needed a darn good reason but a full-fledged permit issued by the *bakufu* itself. Equally strict was the movement of womenfolk. This might sound curious but it made perfect sense under the *sankin kōtai* system. After a year in Edo, a *daimyō* could return to manage his domain but he had to leave his wife and heir behind to serve as hostages. It was a perfect way to keep the *daimyō* in check. The

The Arai Sekisho Barrier as depicted by Utagawa Hiroshige

upkeep of their Edo residences also required a lot of money, money they could not spend on raising a private army large enough to threaten the government in Edo. An important role of the *sekisho*, then, was to make sure no *daimyō* spouses or heirs slipped through the net to reunite with their husbands or fathers at home. If a passport had expired or if it showed up any other inconsistency, its bearer could be turned back to his or her place of departure to have a new one issued. At best—if they had the means and leisure—they would have to spend an expensive month at one of the barrier's inns, waiting for a new passport to be delivered by courier.

Inevitably, there were those who tried to circumvent the barriers, either because their papers weren't in order, because they were carrying firearms without a permit, or because they wanted to smuggle a lover (often a prostitute) back into their domain. The risks of doing so were considerable. Barriers were manned by large police squads who would comb the countryside if word was out that the barrier had been breached. If the culprit was a man, he would be crucified there and then. If they were of the fairer sex, they would be sold into slavery.

There are numerous anecdotes of such illegal barrier crossings, both successful and unsuccessful. Perhaps the most notorious and largest one occurred just three years after Siebold's Mission passed through. It was in 1829 that Honda Masatoki was on his way back to Edo after he had served his term as governor of Nagasaki. As was the custom, he was accompanied by a large number of retainers. The latter seemed to have developed a great fondness for Nagasaki's *geisha*, so much so that no less than twenty-five of them conspired to smuggle six of the damsels across the Arai-*sekisho* by taking a detour through the mountains north of Lake Hamana. They failed. All culprits were caught and put on trial. Two of them were put to death. The others were either imprisoned or placed under house arrest. Four of the women were sold into slavery. The other two made a lucky escape. They had thrown in their lot with a shady merchant by the name of Seizō, who had chatted them up at a previous post town (probably Futagawa) and had managed to procure a small boat by which they safely made it to the other side.

Though strictly maintained during the 17th and 18th centuries, the whole barrier system grew increasingly dysfunctional and porous toward the end of the Edo period when, starved of finances, the *bakufu* did not have the resources to man them. As for the Dutch Mission, it seems that their diplomatic status ensured unhampered passage, even in Kaumpfer's day:

> As to our goods and baggage, they were not opened, but only looked over: only my *atotsuke*, or trunk, which was tied behind the saddle of my horse, met with some difficulty, because of its weight, which made them suspect that there was something extraordinary, and for ought they knew, arms hid in it; but upon some reasons offered them, it escaped being untied and opened. Having been thus searched, we appeared before the shogunal commissioners, who received us with a great deal of civility, and without any difficulty gave us leave to depart when we would.

More than a century later, the Mission with which Fischer traveled passed with equal ease, reasons for which

> The *opperhoofd* went out of his way to pay a visit to the barrier's commander and to thank him for the local lord's lac-quered boat, which was lying in wait for us festooned with a Dutch flag. At the end of half an hour's rowing, we arrived at Maisaka on the opposite shore. We spent the night at Hamamatsu, where we encountered the head of a large retinue of the prince of Owari, who is a close relative of the *shōgun* and is expected to arrive at any moment now.

Hamamatsu

Remarkably, none of our four chroniclers spend many words describing Hamamatsu. Fischer limits himself to mentioning the encounter above, Blomhoff fails to mention the city at all, and even the usually so verbose Siebold has little more to say than that he and the rest of his party arrived late. As usual, Kaempfer has a keen eye for the town's stronghold, but he too is distracted by a procession:

> On the north-side, about the middle of the town stands a large castle, though without any defense, being enclosed only with a thin wall. It being either the yearly fair of the place, or some other holiday, the boys diverted themselves walking in procession through the streets of the town, with drums and other musical instruments, and lighted candles, which they carried upon bamboos.

It seems curious that he should have so little to say about the castle, given that it was once the seat of the founder of the Tokugawa dynasty. But it seems that, following Ieyasu's move to Edo, the town fell into a state of neglect and failed to grow thereafter. Until the early 20th century, that is, when its population exploded from just over thirty thousand to more than a hundred. It was the arrival of the railway that propelled Hamamatsu forward as an industrial city. In 1931, in a bid to attract more trade, the city hosted a Nation-wide Industrial Exhibition. It was a smart move: situated between Tokyo and Osaka, the coast town proved a convenient place for businessmen and punters to meet halfway. The exhibition proved a huge success, attracting more than half a million visitors in two months.

By the end of the 1930s, Hamamatsu had grown into an important industrial hub that, as Japan entered the Second World War, was increasingly geared toward the war industry. And thus Hamamatsu's success spelled its doom, for the presence of industrial plants like the Nakajima Aircraft Company and Suzuki Motors did not escape the attention of Admiral Curtis LeMay and his XXI Bomber Command. Multiple air raids, involving more than five hundred B-29

Hamamatsu City toward the end of WWII

Superfortresses dropped some three thousand tonnes of fragmentation and incendiary bombs on Hamamatsu. The fifth and final air raid, homing in on the city center, was the deadliest. Its incendiary bombs unleashed a firestorm that killed close to two thousand and destroyed most of the city. The little that remained standing was blown to smithereens on July 29, when a flotilla of Allied warships (among them the battleships USS *South Dakota* and HMS *King George V*) made Hamamatsu one of the few Japanese cities to have been subjected to a naval bombardment.

With thirty thousand houses destroyed and its industry in tatters, the road to recovery was long and hard. But determined to build a better future, the Hamamatsuans picked up the pieces. One of them was a young man by the name of Sōichirō Honda (1906–91). Sōichirō, who came from humble beginnings (his father was a bicycle repair man, his mother a weaver) started out as a bit of a delinquent, albeit an inventive one. Uninterested in school, he skipped most classes. When the time came for his father to confirm he had seen the negative school report with his family seal, the boy forged it by crafting a rubber stamp from a piece of bicycle tire. It worked. But only by a stroke of good luck, for the young forger wasn't aware the seal had to be in mirror image. It wasn't a problem with his family name (本田), since its characters (placed above each other) appeared symmetrical; but when friends with asymmetrical names began to place orders too, his little scheme fell through. And so, at the age of fifteen, Sōichirō left home to seek his luck elsewhere. He ended up in Tokyo, landing himself an apprenticeship at a small garage. He returned to Hamamatsu six years later. There he founded Tōkai Seki, a small company that made piston rings for the Nakajima Aircraft Company. Allied bombs destroyed his company. What was left, he sold to Toyota for the sum of ¥400,000—a lot of money in those days. He used it to found the Honda Technical Research Institute. The first fruit of its research was a motorized bicycle, driven by a tiny mass-produced Honda engine. The rest, as they say, is history. Honda Motor Co., Ltd. has grown into a multinational conglomerate that, with an output of 14 million units a year, is the largest manufacturer of internal combustion engines in the world—perhaps not such a positive feat from an environmentalist's perspective. Yet it is thanks to men and women like Sōichirō, that Hamamatsu is now a modern and vibrant city, whose 800,000 Hamamatsuans have caused their city to overtake Shizuoka as the largest city in the prefecture.

I spent the night at the 365BASE Outdoor Hostel, a pleasant place geared to outdoor enthusiasts. Situated on the northern perimeter of Naka Ward, it is well away from Hamamatsu's bustling downtown area. For the weary traveler, too sore to walk into town, there is always the Enshu Railway Line, locally known as the Akaden or 'Red Rail' because of its red railway carriages. Being quite weary myself, I hopped on the Akaden at nearby Sukenobu Station and hit the town to sample some of the local delicacies. I wound up at a place serving rectangular *gyōza*, a creative take on a fried dumpling of Chinese origin. So it wasn't really local but delicious nonetheless.

A reason, perhaps, why none of our four chroniclers dwell on Hamamatsu at length might be the nearby Tenryū River, which pours into the Pacific just east of the city. It is a river that appears time and time again in the accounts of travelers as a major hurdle along the Tōkaidō. So too in Kaempfer's account:

> Having rode near two miles we came to the rapid Tenryū River, which then fell down towards the sea in two distinct arms. This river is very broad, the banks being a quarter of an hour distant from each other. Its rapidity is so great, that it will bear no bridges. We forded through the first arm on horseback, and were ferried over the second in flat prows.

Fischer, too, remarks on the difficult crossing and, like Siebold at Arai, on the quality of the sand:

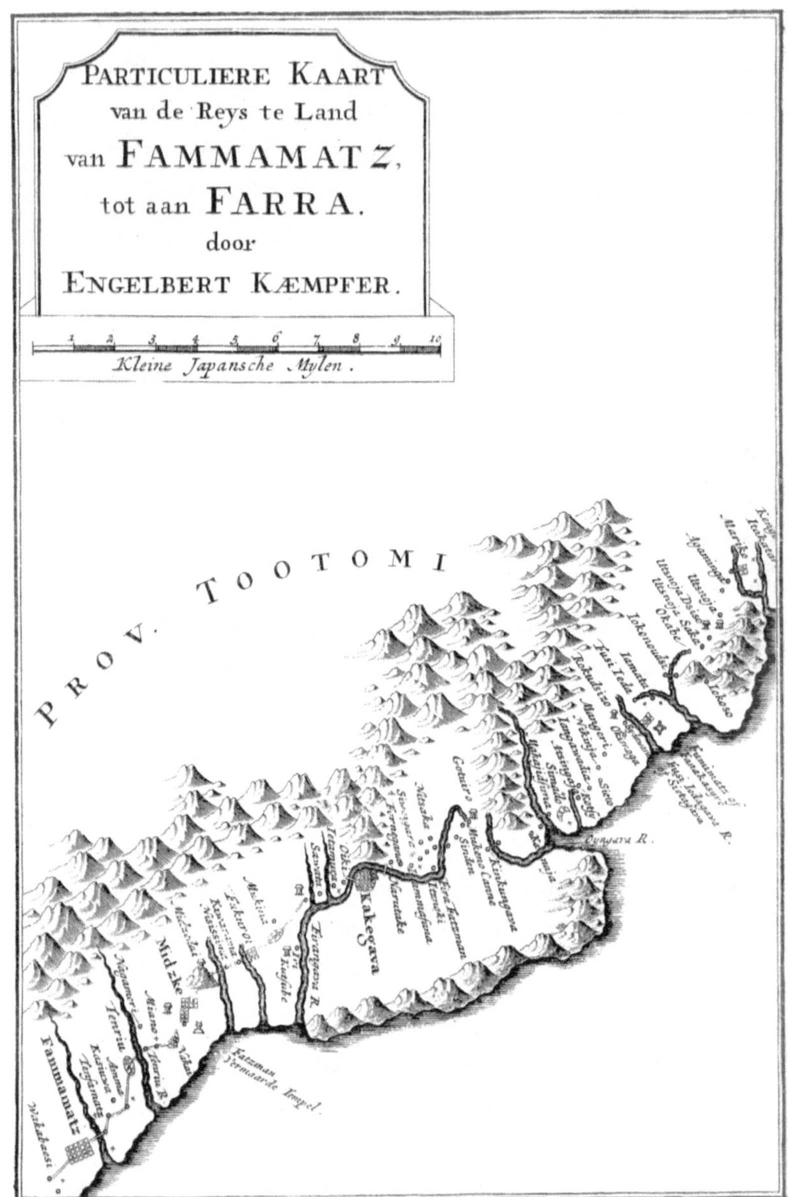

Hamamatsu to Fujieda

On the 19th, we and a section of the handsome retinue we encountered earlier, crossed the fast-flowing Tenryū River. After heavy rains, its banks, or rather its sands, glisten with gold dust, which the Japanese do not yet have the means to extract.

Five huge upstream dams have long since tamed the wild river, and multiple bridges now straddle its wide estuary. For the longest time, right up until and into the 21st century, the river remained a hurdle for the happy few who preferred to follow the old Tōkaidō on foot; for in their pursuit of progress, the authorities failed to fit either of the two bridges that now span the river where one once had to take ferry with a sidewalk, forcing pilgrims to share the road with trucks, busses, and cars alike. The problem was corrected in 2006, when the New Tenryū River Bridge received a wide sidewalk for pedestrians and cyclists. As I crossed the river, I noticed large sandbanks, even islands with vegetation, along its banks and at its center, indicating that, due to the dams, large parts of the river run quite shallow. If one wanted to, one could probably still cross the river in the same fashion as Kaempfer and his party did.

Kakegawa

After dinner, we came to the town of Kakegawa, two miles from Fukuroi. This town has its gates and guards, and a suburb at each end. The castle lies on the north side. It is a large square building, but enclosed only with one plain wall, without any guard houses or other defense. A stately white tower several stories high, adorned, as usual, the middle of the residence.

Kakegawa Castle, which stands on the north bank of the Sakasa River, on the northern outskirts of Kakegawa, is a place well worth visiting, though its main keep is not the one Kaempfer saw; it was rebuilt in 1993 using traditional materials and methods. The result is evident. As soon as one enters the entrance, the delightful scent of *hinoki*, the wonderfully fragrant Japanese cypress, enters one's nostrils, even though the structure has stood for more than thirty years.

At the keep's top floor, I was greeted by Ozawa-*san*, one of the guides on duty that day. The keep's reconstruction in wood, he explained, was the first in the nation. Needless to say, such a project was a costly affair—close to ¥1 billion (roughly $7 million in today's money). Yet not one of those one billion yen came from the government; the entire sum (half of which was used to restore the keep) was raised by Kakegawa's citizens, who at that time numbered just over a million. This means that, on average, they paid just $7 a head—not such a bad deal, really, if you consider what they got in return. Some did a little more than their fair share. Ozawa-*san* walked over to a corner of the room and retrieved an old photo album. Leafing through it, he stopped at a jaded sepia image of an elderly widow by the name of Shiraki Hanae, who alone donated ¥500 million.

Another attraction that makes the castle special is that, along with Nijō, Kōchi, and Kawagoe, it still has a *goten*, or 'castle palace,' which survived the onslaught of the Meiji period and the Second World War. The *goten* dates back to 1861, when it was rebuilt in the wake of the 1854 Tōkai earthquake, which destroyed most of the castle and its original keep. Being a time of peace, fire was the main threat to a castle during the Edo period; often situated at the heart of the castle town, its forbidding walls and ramparts were impotent in the face of even a simple domestic accident as an upset stove. The same

192

Inside the keep of Kakegawa Castle

such accident occurred when Kaempfer and his party passed through Kakegawa:

> A poor man, an inhabitant of the town, sitting with his domestics under the door of his house, a large kettle, wherein they were boiling oil out of some fruits, accidentally took fire, which in an instant set the house all in a blaze, and the wind blowing hard, the flame was instantly communicated to the neighboring houses. We did not take notice of any fire behind us, but perceiving only a thick smoke coming upon us, which quickly covered the sky, we began to be apprehensive of a sudden storm, and to look for our cloaks. But the wind blowing upon our back, soon involved us into such a cloud of smoke and heat, that to escape being suffocated we were forced to ride on a full gallop, and to get as fast as we could out of the way. Being got some hundred paces from the town on a little eminence, we looked back, and saw the whole town all covered with smoke and flames, that we could perceive nothing but the upper part of the castle tower arising, as it were, out of a thick cloud. However, upon our return from Edo, passing again through this place, we found the misfortune less than we apprehended, for the castle had received no damage, and more than one half of the town was saved, although there were no less than two hundred houses, chiefly along the middle and great street, that lay in ashes.

A more personal calamity for the Dutch occurred a century later. It was something Fischer still recalled a few decades after it happened, just after he, too, had witnessed the effects of a large conflagration:

194

Arriving in Mitsuke, we found more than half of the place burned down; only fire-proof storehouses remained here and there. That afternoon we had lunch at Fukuroi and subsequently passed through Nagorie, where they make many colorful mats. And we passed through Kakegawa, where *Opperhoofd* Gysbert Hemmij died in the year 1798; his remains were committed to the earth at the Tennen Temple.

Little is known about Gysbert Hemmij (1747–98), just one among dozens of factors who passed through Dejima in the course of two and a half centuries. He arrived in Japan in 1792 and had traveled down to Edo five times before. When he met his end at Kakegawa, Hemmij and his Mission were on their way back from Edo, where he had had an audience with *Shōgun* Tokugawa Ienari.

It is not clear, either, what caused the demise of the fifty-one-year-old Hemmij, but it did send tongues wagging back at the Dutch trading post at The Cape of Good Hope. It was from there, after all, that, on Tuesday, 3 July 1772, the young merchant had sailed for Batavia aboard the VOC merchantman *Huis ter Meijen* to serve as an assistant to the VOC's Amsterdam Chamber. He did not serve long. He was fired even before the ship arrived when, during a long call at Palembang, he was caught engaging in an illicit trade with the natives. Two decades later, he was hired again and sent to Japan to serve as Dejima's new factor. Now he was dead, cause unknown. Some cried poison; others argued food poisoning; others yet shrugged their shoulders at early old age in the Orient. Whatever the reason, the factor's funeral was a low-key event, the only ones in attendance being the company doctor, its bookkeeper, and a sprinkling of Japanese interpreters.

It was just a short stroll along the Sakasa River to the Tennen Temple. I could not find the grave but an elderly man pruning trees in the temple's courtyard recalled and guided me to it. It was a rectangular tomb in European fashion, large enough to contain a coffin. The heavily withered engraving on the tombstone read:

Here rest the mortal remains of the honorable gentleman Mr.

Gysbert Hemmy's grave on the grounds of the Tennen Temple

Gysbert Hemmy, in his venerable life the Chief Merchant and Factor of Japanese trade, born on 16 June 1747, died 8 ditto 1798, and buried on 9 June 1798.

There he lies to this day, at the Tennen Temple, in the shadow of Kakegawa Castle, under a sky filled with the playful cries of infants from a nearby kindergarten. It wasn't a bad place to rest, really.

196

Sunpu

Just how frequent town fires occurred during the Edo period was borne out when, having just set out from Kakegawa and, having crossed the Ōi River, the Mission with which Fisher traveled learned that their itinerary had been upset by yet another fire:

> We arrived early at Shimada, only to receive the news that we would not be able to spend the night at the place of our destination, Fujieda. We were told it had been visited by a fire that had reduced some three hundred houses to ashes, which indeed transpired when we passed through it the next day, 21 March.

Unable to stop at Fujieda, the Mission was forced to move on to Sunpu (present-day Shizuoka), according to Fisher, 'a famed factory of all kinds of fine weave-, turn-, and lacquer-ware, as well as baskets and boxes artfully crafted from bamboo and wood.'

Sunpu was much more than just a factory of wicker- and lacquerware. It was the place of retirement of Tokugawa Ieyasu after he had yielded the realm and his headquarters of Edo Castle to his son Hidetada in 1605. In truth, he tightly held on to the reins of power. And not even from behind the scenes. Though well into his sixties, he continued to plot and strategize on how to control west Japan's *daimyō*. And when, in 1614, they and Toyotomi Hideyori rose against him once more at Osaka, he rode out from Sumpu at the head of a huge army to join his son in the siege.

Ōgosho, or Great Old Imperial Palace, as he was known in retirement, spent his twilight years in pursuit of his favorite hobby:

falconry. It was more than just a hobby; it was a passion. It was also a way to stay fit or, as he tended to put it, 'keep the bowels moving, stir up a healthy appetite, and secure a good night's sleep.' He had learned the craft from the court noble Konoe Sakihisa, a close friend of Oda Nobunaga and an authority on falconry. Sakihisa was the author of the *Ryūzan kōtaka hyakushu*, a detailed manual on the finer points of handling a falcon, copies of which he gifted to both Hideyoshi and Ieyasu. Hardly a week passed in which the old warrior did not ride out from Sunpu Castle, a long train of falcon whisperers, servants, and womenfolk in his wake. His favorite stomping grounds were around Fujieda, along the banks of the Seto River. Whilst out hunting, he was often joined by men who mattered. Honda Masazumi, for instance, his chief of staff during the Osaka campaign and another keen falconer. It was the equivalent, really, of today's golf: a good way to maintain business relations yet keep the bowels moving, stir up a healthy appetite, and secure a good night's sleep.

Ironically, it was in pursuit of his passion near Fujieda that, on 8 March 1616, Ieyasu became unwell. The diagnosis by his personal physician was food poisoning. It had been on the eve of his fatal outing that the Ōgosho had enjoyed a hearty meal of sea-bream *tempura* finished with a sprinkling of chopped chives. Ever since, he had been plagued by stomach trouble. One wonders whether he would have indulged so much had he not planned on going hunting the next day.

Transported back to Sunpu Castle, Ieyasu lived for three more months. At first, he recovered, pottering about in the castle's recently completed *goten* and spending quality time with his tenth son Yorinobu, who had become the official lord of Sunpu Castle in 1609 at the age of seven. But after a few weeks his condition worsened. He grew weaker with each day until, toward the end of May, he had to take to his bed. Only once did he rise again, to be hoisted in court robes; it was to receive the honor of being appointed Daijō–Daijin or Chancellor of the Realm, an honor Japan's emperors bestowed on only three men before him: Taira Kiyomori, Minamoto Yoshimitsu, and Toyotomi Hideyoshi. Ieyasu passed away on 1 June 1616, the

Sunpu Castle, now the headquarters of the Prefectural Police

exact hour unknown. His remains were buried at the foot of Mt. Kunō, just a few miles east along the coast from Sunpu Castle.

The west section of Sunpu Castle's third bailey is now the domain of the huge offices of the Shizuoka's Prefectural Offices and Prefectural Police Headquarters, whose high-rise buildings tower over the stronghold's recently restored East Gate. The second bailey and inner citadel have merged into a large green area known as

Sunpu Castle Park. Except for the gate and two turrets at its southwest and southeast corners, no castle buildings remain; but walking its vast grounds, you can still feel the original scale of the stronghold. At its center, on a stone pedestal amid a raised paved platform, stands a bronze statue of a rather stocky Ieyasu, his shoulders thrown backward, a falcon perched on his extended left hand, his right hand clutching a battle fan.

Satta Pass

Some ten miles north along the coast from Shizuoka lies the western entrance to the Satta Pass. Looking up at the pass from below is sure to bring a tear to the eye of even the most hardline modernizer, especially those familiar with Hiroshige's wood prints of the famed pass. I had to make my way along a narrow service road along the tracks of the Tōkaidō Main Railway Line to reach its foot. I sought in vain to blot out the cluster of dilapidated sheds of rusty corrugated iron that obscured the view of what is now a sad hill clad in concrete. My eardrums, meanwhile, were being assaulted by the double-barreled roar of the Fuji-Yui Bypass and the Tōmei Expressway, whose high steel fence obscured Hiroshige's splendid view of Suruga Bay. It was just so gut-wrenchingly awful.

It was already in a fittingly mournful mood, then, that I passed through the graveyard that gave access to the first flight of steps toward the pass. From atop the concrete-clad mountain, I could peek over the barrier and saw that there was no longer any white beach, no rocks, just hundreds upon hundreds—no, thousands—of concrete tetrapods.

The Satta Pass in Hiroshige's day

Today's Satta Pass

But then, as I reached the end of another long flight of stairs, I came upon a clearing and had to catch my breath. There, far in the distance but somehow still so close, was Mt. Fuji, rearing its head through a layer of low-hanging clouds. Even the din below could not distract from that magisterial apparition.

I had reached the top of the pass. It was the third pass I had climbed. The biggest hurdle still lay before me: the Hakone Pass. I was the only one there. Below me, thousands of people on the move bypassed me in a more comfortable mode of transport, their toll paid in ugliness.

From the top of the Satta Pass, all the way to the top of the Hakone Pass, Fuji-*san*, as the Japanese reverently call their dormant volcano, would guide my way along the rim of Suruga Bay. Through the forest of red and white chimneys of Fuji City's paper mills, I furtively gazed at her, towering above their acrid fumes as if it were none of her business. And she in turn, from a discreet distance, silently watched over me as I soothed my aching bones in the bay's cool waters near the old post town of Hara.

Nothing has changed about Mt. Fuji since Kaempfer described the mountain so eloquently more than three centuries ago:

It is of a conical figure, tapering from a large basis, and to all appearance even, that it may deservedly be esteemed one of the finest mountains, though otherwise it be quite barren, no grass, nor plants, growing upon it, and the best part of the year covered with snow, which in the summer season indeed, through the heat of the sun, diminishes considerably, but is seldom entirely melted, so as to lay its top bare. According to the account of persons that went up, there is a large deep hole, or opening near the top, which in former times belched out fire and smoke, till at last the uppermost hill arose, but now it is filled with water. Its top being almost perpetually covered with snow, and there being constantly some flocks of it blown off on all sides, it looks in high winds, as if it were covered with a hat of clouds and smoke. For it must be observed, that it is seldom calm at the top, for which reason people ascend it for religious purposes, there to worship their Aeolo, or God of the Winds. They are three days going up, but say, that they can come down again, if they please, in three hour's time, by the help of sledges of reed, or straw, which they tie fast about their waste, and so glide down over the snow in winter, and over the sand in summer, it being, as has been observed, surprisingly smooth and even. The *yamabushi*, or mountain priests, are of this order of Aeolo, and their watchword is 'Fuji-*sama*,' which they frequently repeat in discoursing and begging. Poets cannot find words, nor painter's skill and colors, sufficient to represent this mountain, as they think it deserves.

While I rested on a bench at the top of the pass, an elderly couple overtook me. But when I packed up and continued on my way, I ran into them again: they were coming back. The pass was impassable, they nodded solemnly. Parts of the path had been washed away. I went on nevertheless. I had already passed the high point and wasn't going to let a little landslide force me to go all the way back and make a massive detour. I also did not have the stomach to take in a second time the horrors I had just seen. Besides, I had lived in Japan long enough to know how obsessed the Japanese are with safety. The slightest chip off a building or dent in a road is enough cause to place guards in uniform at either end armed with light-emitting batons to

View of Mt. Fuji from atop the Satta Pass

help the passerby take the frightful hurdle unharmed. And sure enough, in the end, the makeshift fence that had been put up almost proved a greater hurdle than the landslide itself. Only half of the path, over a length of just a few yards, had been washed away; the remainder was perfectly passable.

Coming down at the other end of the pass, I walked along slopes covered with trees bearing oranges. There were also trees bearing

The road was 'impassable'

small, orange, plum-shaped fruit I hadn't seen before. I tried one. It tasted sweet and had the texture of a lychee. For a moment I worried I had eaten something poisonous but a bit farther on each fruit was carefully enveloped in a little wax paper cover. It probably wasn't to keep people from being poisoned.

And yes, a bit farther down the road I met a man in a worker's uniform carefully picking the fruit one by one with a trash grabber

206

and placing them, wax cover and all, in a bucket he wore on a belt over his shoulder. 'What fruit are they?' I asked. 'They are *biwa!*' he beamed. They were loquat. He picked one of the fruits from his bucket, tore open its paper cover, and gave it to me to eat. 'They fetch a hundred yen each,' he smiled. This one was even more delicious. Unlike the previous one, which hadn't been covered, it had a velvety skin. I wanted to cast its piths into the bushes but he stopped me and made me put them in the wax cover and stow them away. 'In that way, people won't be tempted to pick them.' he said. 'If they see the piths scattered around they'll think it's a free for all.'

Yoshiwara

I spent the night at the Running Bare Hostel near Fuji's JR Station. I wasn't running, let alone bare, but it didn't matter, as no one manned the reception desk. In fact, there wasn't even a reception desk. One had to check in by punching in a passcode sent by email upon booking. It was a nice place, really; a small communal area with some furniture, the usual bunks with curtains, and newly fitted showers and toilets. It was the closest affordable thing I could find near the old post town of Yoshiwara, the place where almost all Dutch Missions spent the night before traveling on to Hara if they were coming down from Kyoto, or on to Kanbara if they were going up.

I had just installed myself on the couch in the empty communal area when there was a tap on the sliding door at the front. A young man in his thirties in shorts was having trouble unlocking the door with his password. I slid the door open and let him in. For a moment I thought he was foreign—he spoke such good English. But no,

Hayakawa-*san* was Japanese. He worked at the HR department of a large university in the Kantō region and had taken a long leave to travel around Asia. Now he was back in Japan and going up the Tōkaidō. I was dead tired, but we decided to hit the town after I had had a nap and somewhat recovered myself.

Walking into Fuji's downtown area that evening was a sad experience, another case of *shattaa-dōri*, even more serious than the

The view from Yoshiwara little over a century ago

one at Kuwana; it was terminal, really: hardly a shop or restaurant was open, all shuttered off by the grim face of corrugated iron. I was glad I had company; to walk these streets alone would have been even more depressing. Hayakawa wasn't exactly talkative; he took his time before he spoke, but when he did, it was thought through and made sense.

We finally found refuge at Cafe Resutoran Gasuto, one of those sad clones of the American diner. Inspired by the setting, I began to

208

question Hayakawa-*san* on why it was that so much of urbanized Japan was such a sore to the eye. Surely they must have town planners and policies governing city-scapes? The moment I did, I regretted it. Not that he was offended or grew defensive. Far from it. He simply was at a loss how to explain where it had all gone so horribly wrong. One reason he could point to was Japan's unrelenting post-war pursuit of 'modernization.' Another, in his opinion, was the

The view from Yoshiwara today

deteriorating quality of Japan's civil servants. More and more graduates with the talent and vision to improve things were being lured abroad by lucrative job offers from multinationals. Those who remained at home were being snatched up by Japan's four main cartels: Mitsui, Sumitomo, Mitsubishi, Yasuda.

But there was hope. A small group of Japanese academics and intellectuals had made it their mission to turn the ship around. It was an academic from another large Japanese university who set the ball rolling. In the August issue of the high-end literary magazine *Bungei shunjū*, Tokyo University's Emeritus Professor Itō Shigeru published an article titled 'First Publication of the '"Ugly Japanese Landscapes List.'" It was a list of seventy structures and sites that in the view of a specialist panel of academics and architects are a blot on Japan's city-scapes, as well as its international reputation. Among them were

Tokyo's Nihonbashi Bridge

gaudy shopping malls, run-down *onsen* resorts, and castlelated flyovers amid city centers. At the top of the list was Tokyo's Nihonbashi Bridge. Though rebuilt several times, the bridge once was the place where Japan's five major highways converged and has been immortalized in countless wood prints. It wasn't a matter of concern to Tokyo's town planners. Preparing their city for the 1964 Olympic Games, they conceived of the Shuto Expressway, a multilane flyover that covers the bridge, along with the entire length of the Nihonbashi River. It wasn't a one-off lapse. As evinced by Osaka's Kōrai Bridge and countless others, the capacity of town planners to ignore a place's historicity seems endemic.

Itō's article sent shockwaves through the political establishment. Within months of the article's publication, then Prime Minister Koizumi Junichirō made the emeritus professor head of the City Regeneration Strategy Team, its professed goal 'to promote grassroots town planning.' That was two decades ago. The shopping malls still flash their neon lights, dilapidated concrete structures still pollute the once so splendid Kinugawa River Gorge, and the Kōrai and Nihonbashi Bridges still linger in the shadow of flyovers.

Hakone Pass

> In the forenoon we had four miles to go uphill, the ground being for the most part sandy and barren, though in some places not without plenty of reed, and reed grass. My *dōchūki*, or Japanese road book, gives a particular advice to travelers to take care of themselves in this desert and solitary way.

I was interested to learn that Kaempfer, whose journey up and down the length of Japan was a fully arranged package deal, should have carried with him a *dōchūki*. I had learned more about these Edo period travel guides when, traveling up the Tōkaidō some years earlier, I visited the Tokaido Hiroshige Museum of Art in Yui, the first post town east of the Satta Pass. Most of the museum was dedicated to the art of woodprints, in particular those by Utagawa

211

Hara to Odawara

Hiroshige. But a small section of the museum was reserved for the requirements for travel: carrying bags, writing utensils, fire-making equipment, lanterns, and a 'folding cushion,' which looked like a miniature folding chair, on which one could rest one's head without upsetting one's topknot.

Most valuable to the Edo-period traveler—who tended to be on the road for weeks if not months on end—were undoubtedly the *dōchūki*, pocket-sized booklets with maps, drawings, and descriptions of famous landmarks. They were packed with all kinds of other practical information about life on the road: the distances from post town to post town, the prices of lodgings, the food on offer, even the names of the inns' managers. There was of course one for the Tōkaidō, but also for the Kiso Kaidō, as well as most other high roads.

The advice of Kaempfer's *dōchūki*, incidentally, still applied. The western approach to the Hakone Pass was still a desert and solitary way—at least for those who travel on foot. Only small sections of the former high road remained; for most of the climb, I had to share the road with cars, trucks, and busses climbing the pass in high gear, bellowing forth commensurate quantities of exhaust fumes.

One of the few historic highlights on the western approach to the Hakone Pass is the ruins of Yamanaka Castle. Situated halfway up the pass, it was the first stronghold to fall during Toyotomi Hideyoshi's epic 1590 campaign to reduce the Hōjō headquarters of Odawara Castle on the other side of the pass. More than two dozen Hōjō strongholds were reduced in the course of four months by an army said to have numbered more than two hundred thousand men. One might be inclined to wonder what is so remarkable about the ruins, for not a wall remains standing. But it wasn't its walls that made Yamanaka Castle unique. In fact, it didn't have any, just earthen ramparts. It was its deep dry moats that made the castle such a hard nut to crack. Called *shōji-bori*, or 'paper screen moats,' their floors were covered by a checkered pattern of man-high ridges that ran both parallel and perpendicular to the ramparts, thus making movement within the moats extremely difficult. They are now all overgrown and covered by grass, which lends the place the look of a well-manicured English garden.

Reaching the top of the pass around noon, I looked down on Lake Ashi, just as Kaempfer would have done:

This lake is everywhere surrounded with high mountains, which shut it up on all sides in such a manner, that there is no room to apprehend its overflowing the adjacent country. Though the mountains, which encompass it, are of a very great height, yet the top of Fuji-*yama* rises still higher, being seen to the W.N.W. by the inhabitants of Hakone.

By the time I had descended to the lakeside tourist destination of Hakone village, the weather, which had started out fair enough that morning, had turned sour. A stiff breeze now blew coldly across the lake's waters, which were made unsafe by a fantasy three-master that looked to have sailed straight out of *Pirates of the Caribbean*. Though its sails were furled, it miraculously made its way upwind to the harbor. Over the choppy waters, I could hear the amplified voice of a Japanese Jack Sparrow, thanking his honored guests for joining the Hakone Lake Cruise and expressing his fervent wish to welcome them aboard his humble vessel again in the nearby future. I wondered whether the real Jack Sparrow would have approved of all the groveling.

214

Halfway down the pass to Yumoto, I stopped at the Amazake Chaya an old tea house along the eastern approach to the pass dating back to the early 17th century. The clouds were drawing in, the wind blew harder, and it began to drizzle—the perfect weather for some piping hot *amazake*, a kind of very sweet thin rice porridge.

In the next-door rest house, a small exhibition told the story of the Hakone Pass and the people who made their living from it. One

Lake Ashi, made unsafe by a veritable pirate ship

display highlighted the important role of the *hikyaku*, or 'couriers,' lean and muscular men who carried letters, money, or small parcels from one place to another. Literally, the term means 'flying legs,' which is not far off as some couriers were known to do the Tōkaidō in less than a week. It would take me three! They were a product of Japan's feudal period. Before that, post along Japan's high roads was largely carried by packhorse. But as the country descended into anarchy, warlords began to send their letters by messengers on foot along secret routes so as to escape enemy scouts. They survived up until the end of the Edo period, by which time they had been organized into guilds that protected their interests and sought to ensure their safety.

Hikyaku came in various flavors. *Machi-bikyaku*, or 'town couriers,' did just that, they carried messages from door to door within the

Edo-period hikyaku

metropoles of Edo, Kyoto, and Osaka and were used by officials, merchants, and private persons alike. *Daimyō-bikyaku*, by contrast, only ran for feudal lords. *Tsugi-bikyaku*, last but not least, carried the official messages of high-ranking *bakufu* officials. They were a tough crowd, especially those who plied their trade along Japan's highways. Naked except for a thin loincloth, a head towel, and straw sandals, they weathered wind or rain, heat or cold until, at a young age, their muscles and joints worn out by constant wear, they had to settle into a more sedentary job, often at one of the post stations from which they operated.

I had done this side of the pass four years before, but then I had been climbing, traveling in the opposite direction. Now I flew down the steps like a veritable *hikyaku*, my pace only slackened by the moss on stones turned slippery with rain.

Yumoto's Yasakayu

Yumoto

I had made it to Yumoto, a mountain village tucked away among the northern slopes of the Hakone Mountains famous for its hot springs. This time round I wasn't going to miss out on a good soak.

At just ¥650, the old-fashioned Yasakayu was just my cup of tea. It had only one tiled round tub and two faucets to wash oneself, but

I didn't care tuppence. After all, it was fed by the same healing waters that sustained the high-end places. After more than an hour all the aches had vanished and I felt reinvigorated.

Downhill from the Yasakayu, stood the Sōun-*ji*, the temple where Hideyoshi set up his makeshift headquarters during the siege of Odawara Castle. He too was attracted by Yumoto's hot springs and spent much of his time between war councils indulging in lavish

The Sōun Temple, once the makeshift headquarters of Toyotomi Hideyoshi

parties that started out on the temple grounds and ended up with lots of dilly-dallying in Yumoto's hot springs. He had his whole ménage brought over from his Jurakudai Palace in Kyoto and invited over cronies from the capital to entertain them as they sat out the long wait for Odawara Castle to finally fall. These weren't ruffians either. Far from it. Among them were cultured men like Hon-inbō Sansa, one of the country's best *go* players. Another celebrity was

218

Hon'ami Kōetsu, a man who started out as a sword polisher but climbed the social ladder through his mastery of other arts like calligraphy and painting. Most famous among them was the tea master Sen no Rikyū, who had not yet fallen out of favor with the *taikō* (and forced to commit *seppuku*) and was called upon to prepare him and his guest tea at the Sōun Temple.

A drizzle continued to descend as I walked around the temple grounds. It strangely felt as if the temple was still in denial of its hallowed grounds having ever been desecrated by Hideyoshi and friends. Not a single trace betrayed the *taikō's* one-time presence. Instead, the temple professed its enduring loyalty to the Hōjō and their patriarch after whom the temple is named. A wooden signpost within the temple grounds read:

> The Sōun Temple was built by Hōjō Ujitsuna in the first year of the Taiei era (1521) in accordance with the dying wish of his father, Hōjō Sōun. Ever since, it has been the place where incense is burned by members of the Hōjō clan [in honor of their ancestors] and which, along with their ups and downs, has survived to this day. Many cultural assets that carry the fragrance of Hōjō culture have been preserved at this temple, making it an indispensable temple in its transmission.

To the Hōjō, Hideyoshi's occupation of the Sōun Temple was a double-barreled insult: not only was he laying siege to their castle, but he did so from the very grounds of their ancestral temple. From that perspective, it was understandable that the temple's monks preferred not to remind themselves of the embarrassing episode, let alone remind any visitors it had ever taken place. Was it perhaps for that reason that Kaempfer, who also visited the temple, came away with a rather innocuous, unrelated anecdote, one he couldn't even bother to relate in full:

> Behind the village is the Sōun Temple, and two *Jizō* temples within it, with some *Jizō* columns standing before them. Near one of these temples, they show upon a stone the miraculous impression of the right foot of a son, who with great courage and magnanimity revenged the unjust death of his father. The story, or rather fable, doth not deserve to be here inserted.

Call me stupid but I did think it an interesting story. I combed the temple grounds in search of the mysterious stone with the footprint but could not find it. Having soaked at the Yasakayu until late in the afternoon, I was also too late to ask. Monks inside were already packing up, closing the shutters with such force that I felt too intimidated to interrupt them. It seemed they didn't want to be invaded by unwanted guests a second time around.

Odawara

> A quarter of a mile from this village, and about half an hour after four, we came to Odawara no Ichi, or the suburbs of the town of Odawara, which is most pleasantly seated not far from the sea. The suburbs begin upon the very banks of the river, which arises from the lake of Hakone, and discharges itself into the sea, not far from there, having finished its course between pleasant mountains and green hills, which extend as

far as Odawara, and are washed on one side by the sea, ending on the other into a large plain about a German mile long, on which the town stands. The town is well defended with strong gates and guard houses, ornamented with handsome structures on each side. The streets within are broad, neat and regular, particularly the middle street is remarkable for its largeness. The town is longer than broad, and it is full half an hour's

Odawara and its castle

riding from one end of the suburbs to the other. It reckons about a thousand small houses very neatly built, white washed for the most part, with square court yards before, and curious gardens behind.

On the north-side of the town stands the castle and residence of the prince, which presents itself, as usual, by a beautiful high tower.

Kaempfer's description of Odawara is vaguely reminiscent of an account by another traveler who passed through the castle town guarding the eastern entrance to the Hakone Pass, albeit more than a century earlier. In 1551, Tōrei Chiō, a monk from the Nanzen Temple in Kyoto, made similar observations:

> The town's lanes and alleys are wide and spacious without even a trace of rubbish. Toward the southeast lies the sea, which reaches all the way up to the castle town. His lordship's castle is tall, stately, and a marvel to behold. It is surrounded on three sides by moats that are so tranquil that one cannot fathom their depths.

Odawara still felt spacious and clean, the waves still lapped at the town's outskirts. And I too had trouble fathoming the depths of the castle moats, though it was more down to their murkiness.

I ate some sandwiches in the shade of a cluster of stately pine trees amid the Honmaru Square, the stronghold's former inner citadel. A small cage at its center, in which a sad group of macaques lunged around in boredom, was the only dissonant in an otherwise splendid morning amid historic surroundings. The three-story keep might be a post-war steel-reinforced concrete recreation (and not even a truthful one) but its gabled roofs were still enough to transport one back to a time when they knew how to build such structures. They still did, actually, for the more recently restored Akagane and Umadashi gates have been done using traditional materials and methods.

The weather had turned. The sun was out again, and though it was still early hours, the temperature was rapidly climbing. I wanted to go for a swim but feared a visit to the town's tiny remaining stretch

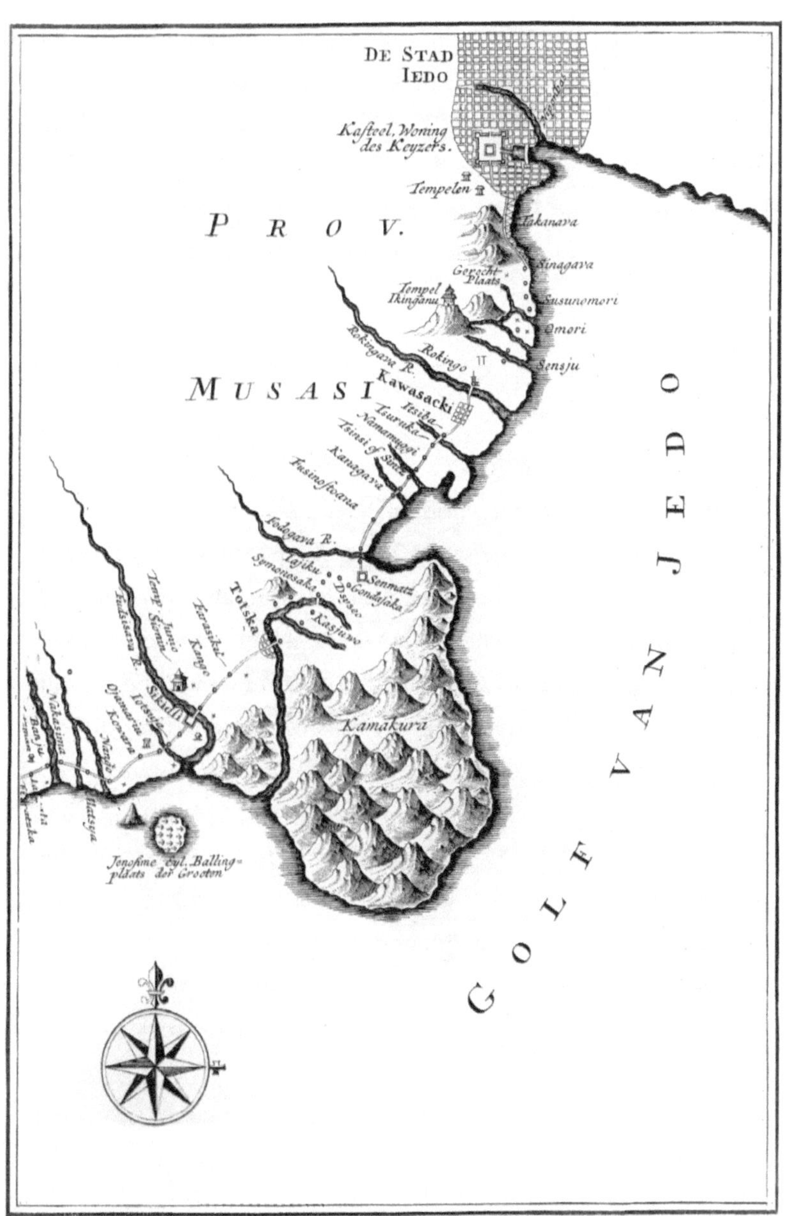

Chigasaki to Edo

of beach would turn out to be the same kind of disappointment as at Suma no Hama. Besides, I had some distance to cover. My destination for the day was Kamakura and the nearby island of Enoshima at the opposite end of Sagami Bay. Better wait till I got there. There would be more sand to enjoy and it would be a nice reward after a long day of walking.

Enoshima

> A mile on this side of Yotsuya, opposite to the village of Kowada, there appears, not far from the coast, a very singular rock arising out of the sea in form of a pyramid, and about a mile off the coasts, directly south, lies the famous Island [of Enoshima and the town of] Kamakura, which signifies 'pillow.' It seems to be round, small, not above a mile in compass, full of timber, otherwise flat; the coasts only are extraordinary high, so that we could see them at a considerable distance. The *shōgun* confines here some of his disgraced noblemen, who, when once sent to this island, may be sure to spend there the remainder of their life. The coasts are steep and rocky, like those of the island Hachijō, and there being no ascent round the whole island, the boats, which bring prisoners, or provisions, must be hauled up, and let down again by a crane.

Of course the area around Enoshima has changed drastically since Kaempfer's time—even since the Meiji period, when old photographs show a coast as yet unspoiled by concrete, steel, or tarmac. Today, the National Highway Route 134 skirts the beach atop a concrete sea wall. Behind it, Enoshima's high-rise apartment blocks with a view of the island stand shoulder to shoulder. Access to the island itself has been 'improved' with the Enoshima Ōhashi, not yet the kind of suspension bridge to Awaji Island near Akashi but already made out of solid concrete. Things could only get better.

But people were still amusing themselves. Out at sea, I spotted a small sailing boat. Nearby, a few people were windsurfing, and

Enoshima. People were still amusing themselves

children armed with small nets on thin bamboo poles were trying to catch shrimps in the murky water at the mouth of the Kobe River. Underneath the sea wall, an old man was playing a *shakuhachi* flute while out on the beach three young women were trying to set up pop-up tents that kept blowing away amid great hilarity.

The sea was even better on the east side of the promontory on which stands the Rokutennō Shrine. More exposed to the wind, this side had a nice surf too. A bunch of young guys in wetsuits prostrated on surfboards were peddling out to sea. I took off my shoes and shirt and also hit the surf. It was wonderful. I let myself drift in the cool water until all the aches in my muscles had gone. I looked back and as far as I could see, all the way up until Cape Inamura, I was the only one swimming. Could it be that the sea hadn't yet officially opened?

Kanagawa

> Kanagawa consisted of one street of about 600 houses and was near half a mile long. Though it has the name of a river, yet there is none that runs through it. The Inhabitants have all their drinking-water from some wells dug at the foot of a mountain or rather long hill at the end of the town. It is clear, but tastes somewhat brackish. The coasts hereabouts appear at low water to be a soft muddy clay.

Unlike Kaempfer, Siebold had little to say about the latest village he was passing through. Odawara, too, had just been 'quite a large city, with gates at both ends, a few shops, and open-ended houses from which beauties in dressing downs glare at us.' Was it because, close to the Mission's goal of Edo, he was growing tired of seeing yet another village, yet another temple, yet another shrine? Perhaps that was why he remembered Kanagawa as the place where he came face to snout with a Japanese bear:

> It was pitch black, had a small and tapering head, a deeply fur-
> rowed brow, a short and pointed snout, but brown flanks.

The animal was four feet long, shapelessly thick, eighteen years old, of which seventeen in captivity, very tame, and performed several tricks.

There is a wonderful photograph of Kanagawa from the end of the Edo period. Its author was a foreigner, not the Italian-born Felice Beato, perhaps the best-known foreigner to capture late-Edo-period

Piere Rossier's photograph of Kamakura from atop Mt. Gongen

Japan, but a man from the Swiss town of Freiburg by the name of Piere Rossier. Like Beato, Rossier was sent out to China by a British photographic company to capture the Second Opium War; but unlike Beato, he failed to get attached to the British forces once there. It was on his way to China that, in 1959, he landed at Nagasaki and met with Johan Pompe van Meerdervoort, one of the Dutch teachers attached to the Nagasaki Naval Training Center. To instruct their students in the science of chemistry, Van Meerdervoort and his colleagues also experimented with photography, but their attempts to capture Nagasaki and its people on plate generally met with failure. And so Rossier took it upon himself to initiate Van Meerdervoort's students in the delicate art of the collodion process, helping foster a cadre of Professional Japanese photographers—Maeda Genzō, Furukawa Shumpei, Keisai Yoshio, Kawano Teizō, Ueno Hikoma, and Horie Kuwajirō, among others—who would go on to capture a country that was rapidly changing. To help them along, he ordered photographic apparatus, lenses, and chemicals from a source in Shanghai. In doing so, he also helped lay the basis for Japan's camera industry, one of Japan's many success stories. It is an industry that made a flawless transition from chemical to digital image processing at the turn of the 20th century, though it is now threatened with extinction by the inexorable rise of the smartphone. In 2007, the year in which Steve Jobs was 'Introducing: iPhone 1,' Nikon, Canon, Minolta, Olympus, Pentax and others still churned out more than a hundred million digital cameras a year. That figure shrunk to just under twenty million within a decade. The reason is obvious: today, more than five billion people worldwide have high-resolution photography and film in the palm of their hands. Clearly, the consumer camera seems on its way out. What remains is a niche market of high-end digital cameras for professionals. But who knows? The Japanese have proven a resourceful people, able to adapt to changing tides. Perhaps they will come up with something new.

Hoping to get the same view of modern-day Kanagawa as Rossier, I made my way to the top of what used to be known as Mt. Gongen, just east of Kanagawa Station. Once, a long time ago, it was the site of a mountain stronghold by the same name. It was the headquarters of Ueda Masamori, a former vassal of the powerful Uesugi clan, who had turned against his masters and joined the Hōjō at Odawara in the hope of expanding his territories. Much has changed since then, even since Rossier set up his camera at its crest during the middle of the 19th century. The hill—it is just that, no more than a few dozen feet high—runs east-west, starting out at where the K1 Shuto Expressway crosses the Takino River and terminating where the K2 leaves the course of the Aratama River. During the early Meiji period, the hill was cut in half when Tokyo and Yokohama were connected by rail. More lines were to follow: the Yokosuka Line, the Sonan Shinjuku Line, the Ueno Tokyo Line, the Tōkaidō Main Line, the Keihin Tōhoku Line, and the Keikyū Line—all force their way through a gap just over a hundred feet wide.

I climbed the eastern side of the hill from which Rossier took his photograph but was disappointed to find that it did not offer the view he had. Though largely asphalted, the hill's flattened crest is now the domain of Kogaya Park, and tall trees obscured the view eastward to where the Tōkaidō passed through the stretched-out village. Perhaps it was a good thing. Even if I had had a clear view, all I would have seen were Kanagawa's high-rise buildings, perhaps with a glimpse in between of the K1 Shoto Expressway, which follows the old high road from a respectful distance overhead.

Westward, across the railway tracks, atop the western vestige of Mt. Gongen, shone the whitewashed walls of the Hongaku-*ji*, the temple that had been the temporary residence of the American consul when Rossier set up his camera on its grounds during the last years of the Tokugawa *bakufu*. The reason the consul wasn't located in Yokohama was that, under the 1858 Treaty of Amity and Commerce, foreigners were allowed only to settle in Nagasaki, Hakodate, Hyōgo,

Niigata, and Kanagawa. Yet, as Kaempfer already hinted, Kanagawa proved a poor port of call because of its shallow waters. Situated right along the Tōkaidō, it was also feared that foreigners might be targeted by nationalists who were against what they considered an 'unequal treaty.' That such fears were well grounded was borne out by a string of attacks on foreigners in and around the settlements over the next decades. And thus the *bakufu* began to look for a more remote port of call, and Yokohama soon beckoned. Compared to Kanagawa, it had several advantages: it had deeper waters, it was situated well away from the Tōkaidō, and it was as yet largely undeveloped. To further enhance the safety of its foreign settlers, a wide moat was dug to create an artificial island. Thus it was that, within just a year, the American consulate moved from Kanagawa to Yokohama's Bund. Before long, the English, the French, the Russians, and the Dutch followed suit.

Ōmori

Today, the village of Ōmori is part of Tokyo's Ōta Ward, though the area is still identified by that name. Ōmori as such was not a post town but, situated halfway between the post towns of Kawasaki and Shinagawa, it had a well-equipped guesthouse where travelers could make a brief stop to rest and take some refreshments before they proceeded to the next post town.

The Dutch Mission with which Siebold traveled also stopped at the Ōmori guesthouse, and it was there that they were met by the retired *daimyō* of Satsuma, Shimazu Shigehide (1745–1833) and his second son Okudaira Masataka (1781–1855), the lord of the Nakatsu

Castle and domain on Kyushu's north coast. Like the rulers of the Saga and Kurume domains, the powerful Shimazu were avid students of Western learning and entertained close ties with the Dutch in Nagasaki, especially the widely learned Siebold:

These high-ranking patrons of the Dutch had alighted at the guesthouse where the Mission was apt to take some rest, and after lingering in the anteroom for some time, we had the honor of joining them. Both lords, besides a young Satsuma prince, received us with excellent hospitality. After we had bowed according to Japanese custom, they invited us to seat ourselves on chairs that had meanwhile been brought into the room. Particularly talkative was the eighty-four-year-old *éminence grise*, the lord of Satsuma, a man whom—still in full charge of his faculties and vigorous in body—one would deem no more than sixty-five. In the course of our conversation, he here and there used Dutch expressions and inquired after the names of various objects that drew his attention.

Ending his conversation with our legates, the old man addressed me by name, saying that he was 'a great friend of animals and natural products' and was 'keen to learn from me how to stuff birds and animals and how to preserve insects,' to which I gladly offered my services. At this, he showed me his right hand, which had recently suffered a bacterial infection. A still open sore had been covered with red-lead cream, on whose unsuitable application I commented without offending his personal physicians. I wrote out a prescription for the required substances and offered to forward them at the first opportunity. Thus I sat, Japanese fashion, before the kindly old man when the lord of Nakatsu took me by the hand and clearly uttered the following Dutch words: '*Kom bij my Doktor Siebold, ik dank U voor de ontvangene brieven en geschenken*' [Come join me, Doctor Siebold, I thank you for the received letters and presents].

Just how dramatic the political climate was to change within just a few decades—when Japan was forcibly opened by the West and made

The hamlet of Namamugu during the late Meiji period

to submit to those unfavorable treaties—is borne out by another encounter between foreigners and dignitaries from Satsuma. That encounter took place at the hamlet of Namamugi, only ten miles down the road from Siebold's happy encounter with his old friend.

It was on 14 September 1862 that four British tourists set out from the newly opened port of Yokohama on horseback to do some sight-seeing at the Kawasaki Daishi, the famous temple on Kawasaki's eastern outskirts, a visit believed to bring good luck. Among the party was a certain Charles Lennox Richardson, a merchant who had made his fortune in Shanghai and was making a stopover in Japan on his way home. Richardson happened to be riding up front alongside the attractive Margaret Watson Borradaile when, as they passed through the hamlet of Namamugi, just north of Kanagawa, they ran into the first members of the one-mile-long procession of Shimazu Hisamitsu (1817–87), the stern regent of the young *daimyō* of Satsuma, Shimazu Tadayoshi (1840–97). Yet instead of dismounting and kneeling down along the roadside as local custom dictated, Richardson, who had already gained a reputation as a colonialist bully in Shanghai (he had almost beaten a servant to death), stayed in his saddle. He turned toward his friends, one of whom called out, 'Don't go on, we can turn into a side road!' But Richardson knew better. 'Let me alone,' he replied, 'I have lived in China for fourteen years. I know how to manage these people.'

Then, before they could stop him, he drove his horse straight through the middle of the procession until, having forced his way through the procession's scouts, porters, physicians, bannermen, and pages, he reached the dozen-men-strong bodyguard of armed ace samurai protecting Hisamitsu's palanquin.

Those who are eager to know what happened next, are invited to read about it in all its gory detail in my book *The Namamugi Incident: The Murder that Sparked a War*, though I have a faint suspicion the title already gives the plot away. Suffice it to say that Mr. Richardson did not meet a happy end and that the British launched the already-mentioned Bombardment of Kagoshima. The standoff lasted just two days, but in Japan it is still known as the Anglo-Satsuma War. Evidently, to the Japanese, it was more than any old 'bombardment.'

Tokyo

I arrived on the northeast corner of the intersection between Edo-*dōri* and Chūō-*dōri* on a sultry late afternoon toward the middle of June. The rainy season was fast approaching and a heavy downpour was predicted for later that evening. The sun was still out, but already clouds were gathering toward the west. I knew I had come to the

The signpost marking the location of the Nagasaki-ya

right spot. A modest signboard with the title Remains of Nagasaki-*ya* stood in a small bed with shrubs right up against the granite facade of the offices of Nakahara Securities. It read:

Here was an apothecary Nagasaki-*ya* in Edo period. When the chief of the Dutch trading house in Nagasaki Prefecture visited Edo, his party stayed Nagasaki-*ya*. Dutch medical sci-

234

entists, for example, Dr. Kaempfer, Dr. Thunberg, or Dr. Seybold, joined the party. So, Japanese physicians and academic people, such as Aoki Kon-yo, Sugita Genpaku, Nakagawa Jun-an, Katsuragawa Hoshu and Hiragana Gennai, visited Nagasaki-*ya* to absorb advanced foreign knowledge. The remains of Nagasaki-*ya* is specified as a historic site in Chuo-*ku* because of the rare place to interact with western civilization under the national seclusion.

Well, that was it. I had traveled a thousand miles to end up facing just another notice with poor English. I felt empty, tired, even a bit disappointed, though I knew full well from the start of my journey that, along with all the others, the inn had long since gone. In that sense, it would have been better to travel in the opposite direction, to find Dejima Island at the end of my travels. But of course that defeated the whole purpose. The goal of the Dutch Mission had been to visit the *shōgun* at Edo Castle and I was traveling in their footsteps.

Sadly, Edo Castle, too, was all but gone. I couldn't even visit the Nishi no Maru, the Western Bailey, if I wanted to; it was now the hallowed grounds of the Tokyo Imperial Palace, the permanent residence of Japan's imperial family. Only twice a year—on 2 January (New Year's Greeting) and 23 February (Emperor's Birthday)—the palace grounds are open to the public. But even then visitors get only a paltry impression of Edo Castle's one-time grandeur.

By all accounts, the members of the Dutch Mission, too, were disappointed, especially when they finally came face to face with Japan's secular ruler. Indeed, the expression 'face to face' does not really cover what went down at the inner recesses of the *shōgun*'s palace within Edo Castle's inner citadel.

Having departed from their inn at the break of dawn, the Mission's senior members would set out along the Chūō-*dōri* toward the Nihon-*bashi*, the famous bridge across the eponymous river. Fischer records how they were dressed for the occasion:

The *opperhoofd* at this occasion is wholly dressed in velvet and brings along, carried by his retinue, the Great Pajong, a saber,

Edo Castle's outer moat and the Tokiwa-bashi Go-mon

two *hasami-bako* [traveler's chests] with thick cords and tassels, and for us (the scribe and doctor) each, two more *hasami-bako*, which are carried on long poles by porters. Alongside the *opperhoofd*'s palanquin go double the regular number of servants.

A hundred yards before the bridge, the procession made a right-hand turn to cross Edo Castle's outer moat and enter the Tokiwa-

236

bashi Go-*mon*. This was a double gated complex with a small court with a guardhouse, which gave access to O-Temae, the castle's large northeast bailey where the *shōgun*'s bannermen were required to maintain their Edo residences:

> Having passed across this first enclosure, riding between the houses and palaces of the princes and lords of the empire, built within its compass, we came to the second gate, which we found fortified much after the same manner with the first. The bridge only and gates, and inner guard and palaces were much more stately and magnificent.

Crossing two more moats and two more gated complexes, they entered the *honmaru*, the castle's inner citadel. Covering well over a hundred thousand square yards, its southern section was taken up by the Omote-*goten*, the buildings that housed the offices of *bakufu* government. Behind it, toward the north and sitting at a slight elevation, sat the Naka-*oku* and the Ō-*oku*, the private residences of the *shōgun* and his womenfolk respectively. Just inside the main gate to the inner citadel stood the Hyakunin-*bansho*, the guardhouse of the Hyakunin-*kumi*, or the 'Hundred-men Companies.' It was the castle's elite guard, made up of four companies drawn from various units that had served Tokugawa Ieyasu at different stages in his career:

> We were commanded to wait in this guard-room, till we could be introduced to an audience, which we were told, should be done, as soon as the great Council of State was met in the palace. We were civilly received by the two captains of the guard, who treated us with tea and tobacco.

Oddly enough, the usually so well-informed Siebold seems to have mistaken the guardhouse for the kind of teahouse at which the Mission had called along the way up to Edo:

> Here we were served very bad tea, and the overall furnishing of this taphouse, where one is made to sit on wooden benches covered with red Chinese felt, did not very much impress us.

The Hyakunin Bansho

Blomhoff, a military man, knew what the function of the building was. Yet the self-aggrandizing man, so as not to demean himself, nevertheless decided to embellish the humble structure:

> Near the second bridge stands a guard house for 100 men. It is a clean and very beautiful room into which the *Opperhoofd* was led to somewhat recuperate and refresh himself. Here, the

Hon'ble [sic.] was welcomed by the Governor of Nagasaki
and both ministers of foreign affairs.

Their patience tested for the better part of an hour 'so that the
audience hall could be prepared,' according to Blomhoff, the party
was allowed to pass through the Naka no Mon and enter the
Omote-*goten* to have their audience with the *shōgun* at the Ō-
Hiroma, the Large Audience Hall for shogunal audiences and other
such formal occasions. Here the Mission's members were instructed
to await their audience with the *shōgun* in one of the hall's
anterooms. Once seated, as Fischer reveals, they got a first inkling
that their 'audience' would not be the dignified affair they might
have anticipated:

> We positioned ourselves in a corner of this room, now
> standing up, and now sitting down again on the mats in
> Japanese fashion, yet were continuously spied upon by those
> who passed by this room, since the sliding doors that set it
> apart from the corridor had been taken away. Accompanying
> us were two of the shogunal sleuths who seem to be dispersed
> at certain distances throughout the palace. In turns we were
> visited here by our Nagasaki governor, foreign commissioners,
> shogunal bigwigs, pages, as well as the lord of Hizen, who
> were all very polite. Yet there were also a number of imper-
> tinents, especially some young lads, who would frequently
> come and stand right in front of us unashamedly and, having
> looked us over close by from head to feet, departed again
> without the slightest bow or greeting.

Finally, having been kept in suspension for another hour, the men were ushered into the Ō-Hiroma. The floor of this hall was said to be covered by one hundred *tatami*, reasons for which it was known to the Dutch as the Hall of a Hundred Mats. At its west end, on a slightly raised dais sat the *shōgun*. Then, while the rest of the Mission's members remained seated at the hall's periphery, the *opperhoofd* was instructed to take his place at 'the third pillar,' presumably a distance

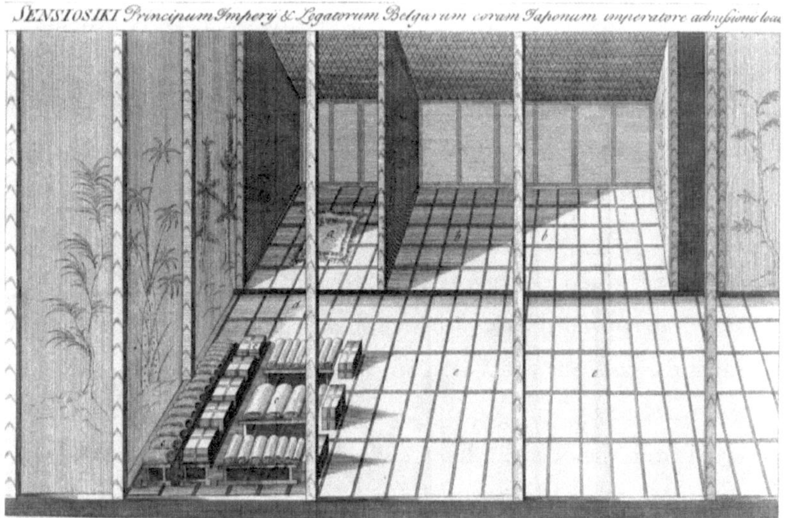

The Ō-Hiroma, alias the Hall of a Hundred Mats

far enough removed for the *shōgun* to see but not smell the unbathed foreigner. According to Kaempfer:

> As soon as he came there, they cried out aloud '*Oranda Kapitan!*' which was the signal for him to draw near, and make his obeisances. Accordingly he crawled on his hands and knees, to a place showed him, between the presents ranged in

due order on one side, and the place, where the *shōgun* sat, on the other, and then kneeling, he bowed his forehead quite down to the ground, and so crawled backwards like a crab, without uttering one single word. So mean and short a thing is the audience we have of this mighty monarch.

More than a century later these formalities had not changed one iota, except perhaps for the order in which the only two words were uttered, at least if we can believe Fischer:

The entire ceremony consisted of making this compliment, in Japanese fashion, at the indicated place, and remaining in that posture for several seconds, with one's head touching the mats, until someone called out, '*Capitan Oranda!*' Except for the quiet rustle of garments by which the Japanese instill profound reverence, a deadly silence reigned. The governor of Nagasaki and the senior interpreter were the only ones who accompanied the *opperhoofd* and gave him the sign that he could leave, and in such a manner that, though one might see a few people, one can not look around to that which would otherwise attract one's particular attention without offending Japanese sensibilities.

Despite its almost dismissive brevity, the audience with the *shōgun* left a deep impression on Kaempfer:

This audience is otherwise very awful and majestic, by reason chiefly of the silent presence of all the counsellors of state, as also of many princes and lords of the empire, the gentlemen

of his majesty's bedchamber, and other chief officers of his
court, who line the hall of audience and all its avenues, sitting
in good order and clad in their garments of ceremony.

The formal audience with the *shōgun* being over, the foreigners
next had to pay a visit to the *shōgun*'s son and heir, who resided in
a similarly luxurious palace on the grounds of the Nishi no Maru,
the castle's West Bailey. For Siebold, this proved even more of an
anticlimax since they did not meet the young man in person but had
to make do with three of his 'councilors of state.' While waiting for
the councilors to make their appearance, he noted how:

In front of us was a long wall of sliding doors whose windows
were covered with thin paper instead of glass. In this thin paper,
small holes had been cut through which we could observe
various parts of court ladies ogling us. Sometimes one could see
the eyes, sometimes one managed to discern a small red mouth,
a part of their hair dress, or the bright colors of their makeup.
In this manner we endured our otherwise awkward situation
and remained, as long as it was required, calmly seated on the
mats with our legs folded under us.

After their audiences at the castle followed at least a dozen more visits
to the residences of officials lower down the *bakufu*'s pecking order.
Yet even these turned out to be less of an occasion than expected,
reason for Siebold not to waste too many words on them, since:

Nowhere did we find the master of the house at home, though
invariably we paid our deep compliments to their secretaries,

let ourselves be broken on the rack, be exposed to curious glances; and again and again be made to smoke tobacco, drink tea, eat sweetmeats, write out maxims, let people look at our curiosities, etc.

Moreover, even on these occasions the Dutch did not get to see their interlocutors but were invariably glowered at from behind the ubiquitous bamboo blinds. It was on one such occasion that the whole peeping-Tom arrangement was upset when:

All of a sudden one of the blinds collapsed, revealing a group of women, who just as suddenly managed to flee, but would most certainly have been held to account for thus upsetting the decorum of our reception.

Coming at the end of a taxing two-*month* journey on horseback or squeezed into cramped palanquins, the effect of all these bewildering, rather demeaning meetings on the Mission's members was best described by Siebold:

Finally, at nine o'clock in the evening, after we had been paraded about in uncomfortable costumes, and had to sit on the floor with our legs folded underneath us during constant bowing, we arrived with upset stomachs and throbbing headaches at our inn—our wretched 'consular residence' does not deserve any other name. Dead tired as we were, we nevertheless had to receive a number of servants of the foreign commissioners who, on behalf of their masters, congratulated us on the success of our audience.

Yet the ordeal was still not over. During a second audience, a few days later, the hapless foreigners were led even deeper into the Omote-*goten*, into the Shiro-*shoin*, the hall used for festivities, to be paraded before the *shōgun*'s consorts, and the 'princes of the realm.' The ensuing scenes seem pulled right from the pages of *Guiliver's Travels*. The truth, of course, is even better; Swift almost certainly based his description of Japan on a prepublication draft of Kaempfer's work.

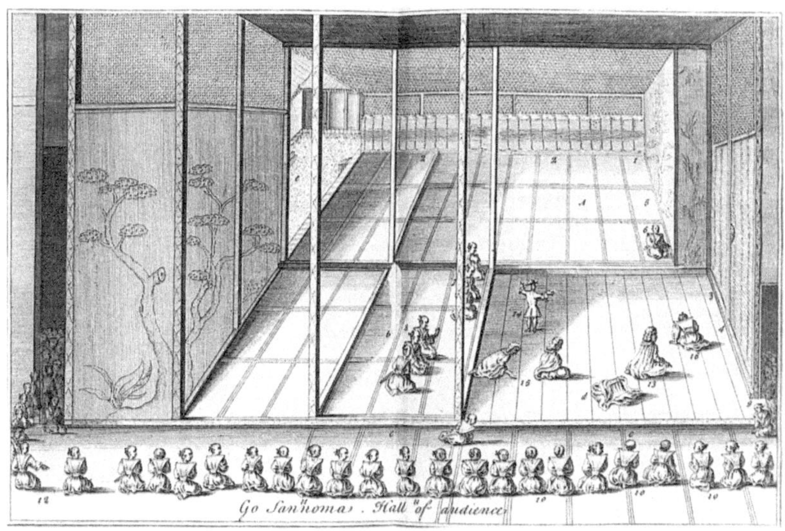

Comic scenes during the second audience

One has the strong impression the German physician is almost embarrassed when he relates how:

We were asked a thousand ridiculous and impertinent questions. Thus for instance, they desired to know, in the first place, how old each of us was, and what was his name, which we were commanded to write upon a bit of paper, having for

244

these purposes taken a European inkhorn along with us. This paper, together with the inkhorn itself, we were commanded to give to Munetsune, who delivered them both into the *shōgun*'s hands, reaching them over below the lattice.

This, however, wasn't enough for the *shōgun*:

Then he ordered us to take off our *kappa*, or cloak, being our garment of ceremony, then to stand upright, that he might have a full view of us; again to walk, to stand still, to compliment each other, to dance, to jump, to play the drunkard, to speak broken Japanese, to read Dutch, to paint, to sing, to put our cloaks on and off. Meanwhile, we obeyed the *shōgun*'s commands in the best manner we could, I joined to my dance a love song in High German. In this manner, and with innumerable such other apish tricks, we must suffer ourselves to contribute to the *shōgun*'s and the court's diversion.

Needless to say that all this frolicking about, was also observed from behind bamboo blinds. But despite these obstacles, Kaempfer still managed to get a glimpse of that which no mortal Japanese was allowed to see:

As I was dancing at the *shōgun*'s command, I had an opportunity twice of seeing the *shōgun*'s consort through the slits of the lattices, and took notice, that she was of a brown and beautiful complexion, with black European eyes, full of fire, and from the proportion of her head, which was pretty large, I judged her to be a tall woman, and about thirty-six years of age.

Those behind the lattices, Kaempfer observed, apparently also found them a hindrance:

> I took notice, that pieces of paper were put between the reeds in some parts of the lattices, to make the openings wide, in order to get a better and easier sight. I counted about thirty such papers, which made me conclude, that there was about that number of persons sitting behind.

All in all, then, the audience with the most powerful man in the realm—Tokugawa Tsunayoshi (1646–1709) in Kaempfer's case; Tokugawa Ienari (1773–1841) in Blomhoff's, Siebold's, and Fisher's—turned out to be somewhat of an anticlimax. Rather than being considered important ambassadors of a foreign power, they felt they were seen as a curiosity, a freak show, to be watched and giggled at from behind the safety of bamboo screens.

Sunk in though, I sighed as I stared at the Nagasaki-*ya* signpost. I was startled from my reveries by a cuckoo sound behind me: the pedestrian traffic lights had just turned green. I crossed the road and bought myself an ice cream at the local 7-Eleven. Then I sat down on a low wall near the intersection to rest my weary body. A red Hop On Hop Off double-decker tourist bus headed for Nihonbashi pulled up for a red traffic light, at the exact same corner where once stood the inn. But I heard no guide announce, 'And here, on your left, once stood the Nagasaki-*ya*, the inn where the Dutch merchants used to stay during their audience with the *shōgun* at Edo Castle.' The foreign tourists on the open top floor of the bus looked in the opposite direction, upward, gazing at the towering heights of the Eslite Spectrum Nihonbashi department store. Down below on the pavement, Tokyoites went about their daily business, pushing strollers, carrying shopping bags, staring at and talking into their smartphones. How many of them, I wondered, knew that once, not too long ago, their fellow citizens had thronged at the inn's latticed windows, hoping to get a glimpse of those strange Dutchmen inside.

TOYO PRess publishes books that contribute to a deeper understanding of Asian cultures. Book and cover design: Chōkei Studios. Editorial supervision: Letitia van der Merwe. Printing and binding: IngramSpark. The typeface is Cardo.